Loved Back to Life

Everything Everyone Needs to Know About Alcoholism & Drug Addiction

Amy "AJ" Crowell, MBA

AJC Media Services
Dallas, TX

ISBN: 1-4196-5604-X
ISBN-13: 9781419656040

Visit www.booksurge.com to order additional copies.

Disclaimer:
The information contained herein is for educational purposes only. It is based upon the consensus of current facts obtained from peer reviewed literature and from the experience of the author. It is not intended to be used for diagnosing or treating any mental or physical disorders. The information presented in this book should not replace the advice of your caregiver or doctor. Always consult your health care practitioner for any concerns related to alcoholism and other addictions.

Published by:
AJC Media Services
1333 W. Campbell Road
Richardson, TX 75080

www.lovedbacktolife.com

Printed in the United States of America

Dedicated in loving memory to my Mother & Father.

SOON TO BE RELEASED

By: Amy "AJ" Crowell

Calm
Cool &
Connected

To positive thinking!

A 365 daily confidence booster to keep your thoughts positive! Amy's new book includes daily quotes, inspirations, affirmations and questions to ponder. It inspires you to reach for your dreams by believing in yourself and seeking the positive in everything.

www.amycrowell.net

CONTENTS

Content Explanation

Loved Back to Life was written to address a wide variety of people including alcoholics and/or drug addicts who are still practicing their addictions, those in recovery and those who are affected by another's alcoholism and addictions. I wrote *Loved Back to Life* to include everything of the utmost importance (in my opinion) about alcoholism and addictions that everyone MUST know in today's society.

The book is divided into 5 distinct sections. Section I consists of Chapters 1-27 reveals my life story from childhood, through alcoholism and drug addictions and into recovery. Section II describes ways that I believe have helped me remain sober including a list of "Do's and Don'ts" for recovery while Section III features the facts about alcoholism and drug addictions and the most commonly asked questions and misconceptions. This section presents three different self-tests to determine if a person may have an alcohol or drug problem to identify codependency issues and to allow parents to sell-assess for addiction. Meanwhile, Section IV highlights five "Sober Success Stories." The stories chosen are personal friends whose amazing journeys show remarkable strength and offer hope to those still affected by alcoholism and drug addiction. Lastly, Section V of this book has a list of places where "Help is Available" for those suffering from numerous types of addictions.

If you have a sober success story, questions or comments, we would love to hear from you. Please go to our website www.lovedbacktolife.com to find free information and join our newsletter. The site is updated continuously and free downloads are also periodically offered so check the site often.

Foreward

About 18 million Americans have alcohol problems; about 5 to 6 million have drug problems. [1]

It is important for me to include my story and the stories of others in this book. When I was first becoming sober, it was a necessity to hear other alcoholics' and addicts' stories. I had to hear their experiences so I knew other people had done the same insanely foolish things that I had.

My very first meeting in alcohol and drug treatment was a speaker meeting and I was told to listen for our similarities. I heard that they shared the same intense feelings of doom and dread that I had, that their unusual thinking patterns were like mine, and we had the same kind of drunken stupors. I was comforted to find that other people could not stop drinking and loved drugs as much as I did. The stories told in speaker meetings brought a sense of relief to me. For the first time in my life, I felt like I actually fit in somewhere. I knew I was in the right place with people who were like me and that was comforting.

The stories in this book are not only for alcoholics and addicts, but for everyone who is dealing with a person in their life who suffers from alcoholism and addiction. The stories will enlighten non-addicts about the realities of the drunken alcoholic and practicing addict. People will begin to understand why alcoholism is classified as a disease by the American Medical Association and realize that unless you have experienced alcoholism first hand then you can never fully understand the disease. However, non-addicts can still be educated and learn to identify with alcoholism and other addictions. More importantly, the stories will reveal how alcoholics and addicts hide their disease and will also act as a guide to determine if someone may need help for his or her addictions. Parents of teenagers will find the information to be an eye-opening experience and it most likely will influence how they handle the topic of alcohol and drugs with their children. It will also educate parents on how teenagers often drink and use drugs without their parents even realizing that addiction is progressing in their own child. On the other hand, teenagers who are abusing alcohol and drugs will also relate to my personal experiences as a teenager. Like many other teenagers, they may discover they are addicted; however, it is safe and vital that they seek help.

It is also imperative non-addicts reading these stories realize many sober alcoholics have survived inconceivable circumstances and are now thriving, even though the stigma of being a "drunk" is often still attached. The inspiring stories found in this book will not only help readers recognize how incredibly fascinating these sober addicts are, but readers will gain respect for sober alcoholics as a whole. Readers will acknowledge and reconsider the negative stigma is attached to alcoholism, and understand how this stigma often lingers even after an alcoholic is sober for many years.

Please Note: *The names have been changed throughout the story so those who do not want to be public can maintain their privacy.*

Section 1

The Story of How Amy was *"Loved Back to Life"*

"It is one of the most beautiful compensations in life that no man can sincerely try to help another, without helping himself."

– Ralph Waldo Emerson

Chapter 1
Alcoholism: The Family Secret

My story is written as if I am telling it to a support group of alcoholics and addicts. I have been taught to honestly tell my journey, strength and hope.

"Hi, I'm Amy and I'm an alcoholic addict. I've been sober since April of 1988."

The group responds in unison, "Hi Amy!"

I smile at my companions and begin my story…

"I took my first drink at 5 years-old sitting on a bar stool with my father at the local Irish Pub in Orchard Park, New York. As he sat next to me drinking his endless mugs of beer, he would put a shot glass of beer in front of me and warned me to drink it slowly. I did not like the bitter taste, but my father and his friends laughed when I drank and I liked the attention. So I drank my beer with a big smile. I felt so grown up and happy to be with my father when he was in good spirits and not raging. These moments were few and far between.

United States alcoholism statistics show that people who start using alcohol before the age of 15 are 4 times more likely to become an alcoholic at some time in their lives, compared to those who start drinking at the legal age of 21.[2]

My father drank beer everyday, so I grew up thinking that most adults did the same. My faithfully codependent mother would often have a glass of wine and join him. Because they both chained smoked, the house smelled like an incinerator. I hated the foul smell of the cigarette butts that filled the ashtrays all over the house. It was something I always found disgusting and I despised it.

Every night when I went to bed, if I had been good, I would be treated to a little "Party!" This meant that I could have a snack of whatever I wanted and my favorite snack was ice cream with Crème De Menthe poured over the top. I loved the coldness of the ice cream and the warm feeling of the Crème De Menthe going down my throat.

So at 5 years old, I was drinking beer at the neighborhood bar and my favorite dessert was ice cream with a liqueur poured over it. My father and both my grandfathers were alcoholics. Meanwhile my mother was 100% codependent and just as ill as my father. Our entire family was sick because of the alcoholism passed down from generation to generation. If anyone was destined for alcoholism, it was me.

More than nine million children live with a parent dependent on alcohol and/or illicit drugs.[3]

I went to a Catholic school for eight years, and I never considered alcohol dangerous. Wine was used in the church ceremony everyday, and they turned wine into the blood of Jesus so I figured that it must be extremely special. The dangers of drinking and drugs were never discussed. These topics were swept under the carpet and they were considered as taboo a subject for discussion as sex. My father, the king of denial, pretended the hippie generation never existed.

Teenagers whose parents talk to them on a regular basis about the dangers of drug use are 42% less likely to use drugs than those whose parents do not.[4]

Going to a Catholic school was not a positive experience for me. It took me a long time to learn that the Catholic religion was not the problem; rather, it was the people that I was surrounded by and my personal perception of the Catholic religion. Needless to say, my perception was rather warped. I completely missed the forgiveness the church teaches. Instead, by the third grade, I was convinced I was going to hell. So, I rationalized, it did not matter what I did...good or bad.

My first twisted experience with a nun, Sister Mary, came in the first grade. It gave me the impression all nuns were going to be exactly like her. One day, I remember having to use the lavatory and Sister Mary refused to let me. I continued to ask her and she yelled at me and told me I had to wait until we all went as a group.

I was so consumed with fear. I would not get up and go without permission. Instead, proceeded to pee in my panties the dribbled down the chair and on my leg. It was so embarrassing and my classmates all laughed while Sister Mary made me sit in the pee-soaked chair and my wet, urine-stained clothes all day. I rode the bus home wearing my formerly white bobby socks that were now smelly and yellow.

I did not cry until I got home and I told my mother what had happened. I knew she would do something to fix it, but to my dismay, she did absolutely nothing. My mother explained to me nuns were special people and if they did something it was for my own good. What I heard her say was the church could do no wrong and she did not care enough to defend me. It was at that moment I began to despise my school and the Catholic Church. It was my first resentment and I fed and nurtured it for many years to come.

Later that year, Sister Mary informed our class rich people went to hell and poor people went to heaven and this perplexed me. We were a group of first graders who mostly lived in affluent areas and whose fathers held prominent jobs so what she was teaching us was very confusing. I knew that we were far from being poor and I pondered whether I was going to hell. I came to the conclusion that what Sister Mary had said was true because my mother had told me that nuns were never wrong. So, I figured I was hell-bound, and I wondered why God hated me so much.

During this time my life at home was unbearable. My alcoholic father was a horrific rager. He would yell and scream at the top of his lungs at my mother, sister, brother and me. He was a big man standing more than 6 feet tall and weighing over 200 pounds. He scared me. He would yell and strategically place his body close to ours and would glare at us while his temper flared uncontrollably. There was no predicting his actions because he would have a rage attack sober or drunk. His ranting and raving at everyone became a common occurrence. The out-of-control craze in his eyes as he was boiling with rage was terrifying.

At a young age, I learned to hide inside my closet. I would get in my toy chest when I heard him coming in the door from work, and I would wait to see what kind of mood he was in. Sometimes his raging would start the minute he walked in, and I would stay in my toy chest for hours.

53% of men and women in the United States report that one or more of their close relatives have a drinking problem.[5]

Because of the dysfunction in my house, I would rarely have friends over to spend the night. I did not know if my father would be drunk or raging or both. I could not bear to let someone find out our family's secret and see how we actually lived.

Untreated addiction is more expensive than heart disease, diabetes and cancer combined.[6]

Once, I invited a friend of mine to the 4th of July fireworks show in town. My father drank beer all night and was drunk by the time the firework show was over. He drove anyway and as we were leaving we got stuck in traffic. My father started yelling at another driver. They ended up getting in a fist-fight and attracting a crowd and the police. My friend and I sat in the back seat petrified. I was humiliated by my father's actions and I feared that my friend would tell other people that my father was a raging, drunken lunatic. The last thing I wanted was for people to find out our family's secret. That was the last time I brought a friend around my father.

Chapter 2
Childhood Secrets

Approximately 12 years old, some of my friends started having drinking parties at their houses when their parents were not home. Raiding liquor cabinets was easy for us. We would take most of the liquor and then fill the bottles back up with water, so our parents would not know.

This was the about same time I discovered boys. I found that kissing and touching boys and vice versa felt wonderful. I experimented with different boys and I liked the attention that they were giving me; I felt special. I never felt special at home, so boys were a new revelation I decided to continue researching.

Even though I was drinking and experimenting with boys at a young age, I looked very normal from the outside. I concealed both my personal and my family's secrets, so very few knew the truth. I was popular at school and had many friends. I learned quickly that the more activities that I was involved in, the less I was at home and amidst the chaos. So I became involved in everything I could: cheerleading, tap, jazz and ballet classes, singing in the choir, girl scouts, horseback riding lessons and the swim team. As a result, I was never home and that pleased me. Away from home I had some semblance of self-confidence, and I found I was good at a variety of activities. This was a complete dichotomy from my feelings while at home. My father reminded me constantly with his verbal and mental abuse that I was stupid and could do nothing right. It felt as if my insides would shrivel up and die at the sound of his voice.

Alcoholism statistics in the United States remain staggering. Sadly, a reported 2.6 million binge drinkers in 2002 were between the ages of 12 and 17.[7]

I was taught at a young age that being attractive to boys would be an extremely important part of a woman's life. When my father had men over to play pool in our game room, he would ask me to serve the men their beer. I was only 7 or 8 years-old, and there I was serving cold beers, in my pajamas, for my Dad's friends while they played pool. Throughout the night, he would joke with the guys and then bet I could beat one of them in a game. Since I practiced playing pool often by myself and sometimes with my father, I could play. Inevitably, I would end up shooting a game with all the men watching. My father would then tell everyone if I *developed properly* I was going to be a Playboy Bunny. Everyone would laugh, except me because I was not exactly sure what he meant. However, I could figure that it meant I had to be beautiful and play pool well. I vied to become a Playboy Bunny because maybe then my father would stop yelling at me. This became my goal so I could please my father.

At about the same age, I went with my parents to visit my grandmother in Cincinnati, Ohio. I liked visiting my grandmother when my mother, sister and I would visit her without my father. We would laugh and have a great time while we were there. It was like we were free to be ourselves without my father around. But, on this one particular visit, my father, mother and I were the only ones who went. We all slept in the same bedroom and I hated that.

One evening, my grandmother was having friends over and I needed to take a bath and get dressed. My father got exceedingly angry at me when I was in the bedroom deciding what to wear. He spiraled out of control in one of his raging tangents and he cursed at me to hurry up. I explained I was getting my clothes so I could put them on in the bathroom, after my bath. He continued his yelling tirade, took my clothes, and instructed me to take my bath. He continued by telling me to walk into the living room naked and ask for my clothes when I was finished. I was appalled because my grandmother's guests were already arriving. I could not believe that he wanted me to prance naked into a room of people. He pushed me into the bathroom and slammed the door shut leaving me without my clothes or a towel. This was the first time in my life that I knew without a doubt that my father was screwed up.

Even at a young age, I knew it was inappropriate of him to demand that I parade around naked in front of a group of strangers. I called for my mother, but she was more petrified of my father than I was. Once again, my sick codependent mother did not come to my defense. She would never have done anything to defy him.

I remember thinking he was a pervert. I did not know what it meant exactly or where I had heard it, but I sat on that bathroom floor crying and thinking my father was a pervert. So eventually, I was forced to walk out naked in front of a room of strangers and apologize to my father and ask him for my clothes. I had never been so ashamed and I have never forgotten that feeling. It was going to be a very long time before I would forgive my father. I refused to let him see me cry so I stuffed all my feelings deep down inside my gut with all my other pain. My resentments were slowly building and festering. They would later come pouring out.

Today my father's actions and behavior would be considered sexual abuse. At the time, all I knew was I felt ashamed, dirty and scared.

Among drug-using women, 70% report having been abused sexually before the age of 16; more than 80% had at least one parent addicted to alcohol or one or more illicit drugs.[8]

Chapter 3
Confused Rebel

In the seventh grade, it was not surprising to me my teachers at school requested a meeting with my parents and suggested that I receive some professional help. I had started acting out my frustrations at school with the teachers and nuns. Since I perceived I was going to hell, I hated religion class with a passion. I threw the bible at the nun one day and told her I was not going to read it or do the assignment. The nun was shocked and probably thought that the devil had taken over my body. If she only knew the devil was disguised as alcoholism, and he had only just begun.

Bad behavior and a smart mouth became part of my personality. It was apparent I was acting out the emotional cruelty I had been enduring for years. My parents told my teachers it was a phase I was going through and it would stop soon. They opted out of getting me any professional help. If they had to get me help, then they would have to admit there was something wrong with the family. Our secret would be exposed and, in those days, dysfunction was not talked about as freely as it is today. Dysfunction in a family was a secret that was kept well- hidden. That is the way it had always been because the dysfunction continued in a vicious cycle decade after decade. No one in my family knew life could be so very, very different.

A dysfunctional family is a family in which conflict abuse, or misbehavior by individual family members take place on a continual basis, leading other members of the family to perpetuate, enable, and reinforce such behaviors. Often children grow up in dysfunctional families with the belief that such behaviors and ways of relating are "normal."[9]

My family became experts at hiding our dysfunction. Most neighbors did not know of the severe family troubles we were having. I rationalized many other families had the same kind of secrets and everyone hid them from each other. We lived in a beautiful house and seemed to have everything monetarily we wanted. My father was very functional and successful at work, and he was continually being promoted. This was mind-boggling because I knew my father was an alcoholic; however, he did not seem to fit the stereotypical alcoholic I saw on television. The people on T.V. drank all the time, lived on the streets or a tiny apartment, and could not hold down jobs. The only common denominator between my father and the stereotype was he drank all the time.

As time passed, I became more curious and my rebellious phase showed no signs of ending any time soon. Since my defiance was in full-force and marijuana was prevalent with many kids in my neighborhood, I decided I would give it a whirl. My first experience was in the 7th grade. My friend took me in the neighborhood woods and I took a few drags from a joint. It was fun and made me feel light-headed and floaty. It felt like nothing really mattered and my troubles temporarily vanished. Afterwards, when pot was available, I was the first in line. Later, I experimented with smoking dope from a bong. Even though I gagged a lot because the bong was harsh and burned my lungs it was a quicker, much more intense high. I liked that feeling of euphoria.

20% of 8th graders report that they have tried marijuana.[10]

In the spring of 1977, my mother and sister told me they needed to talk to me about something important. I knew it was serious because our family never talked about anything. We completely avoided discussions. They proceeded to tell me my father's job had been transferred to Dallas, Texas and we were moving. I hated my father more at that moment than I had ever hated anyone in my life. He had previously threatened to move because that winter Buffalo had been inundated with 200 inches of snow and we were buried in our house. We had no electricity and the National Guard was sent to dig the city out. I looked at it as an adventure and my father looked at it as something that would never interfere with his drinking again. He ran out of beer during this time and it was not a friendly environment in our house. There may have been a mammoth storm outside, but the fury of negativity my father dealt inside the house was far worse.

The worst part about moving was my sister was staying in Buffalo and not going with us. My sister was in her mid-twenties with her own life and was probably grateful that my parents were leaving. My brother had left home at eighteen and moved to Colorado. He rarely came back, not that I blamed him. However, my sister was my saving rock, and I could not imagine living with my parents all by myself. I could not swallow this concept and I sobbed and sobbed and begged to stay with my sister. Living without her and my friends was inconceivable. There was no way I was going to move across the country to some city I had never been with an exceedingly sick codependent mother and a raging abusive alcoholic father. I was sickened with disgust that my parents would even think I would want to go with them.

The reality was it did not matter what I wanted because my father said we were going. Unwillingly, I was going to Richardson, Texas. Once again, my functioning alcoholic father had received a promotion and was going to be working at his company's corporate headquarters. At the time, it baffled me, how he could be successful in business and be such an out of control idiot at home.

Men are twice (21%) as likely as women (10%) to be heavier drinkers (individuals who consume two or more drinks per day on average).[11]

As I was entering this new phase in my life, I did not realize that at fourteen years-old, I would be losing any speck of innocence I still had. My life was changed forever and I felt like I wanted to crawl into a little ball and die. I felt my insides were already dead and I knew I could not continue living in constant fear of my father. I had to find a way to survive.

Chapter 4
Culture Shock

We moved into our new house right before my 9th grade school year. To my relief, one of my neighbors was a girl whose name was Anna. We were the same age and she took me under her wing. I do not know what I would have done without her family at that time. They probably did not realize that by opening their home to me day or night, they were saving me from the misery of my household. I had never felt so alone and out of place, but their generosity made me feel I could endure.

Anna took me to school the first day and explained how it worked. I had never been to a public school and the Catholic school I attended before had only sixty students in each grade. My new junior high had hundreds of kids in the 9th grade and even more in the school. Saying that I was overwhelmed would not have come close to describing the situation. The culture shock I was experiencing had me nearly paralyzed with fear.

I had always been popular and very fashionable back in upstate New York. I wore straight hair pulled back in a barrette, big pull over sweaters and Levi jeans. My shoes consisted of flat clogs and Top Siders. The southern girls at my new school looked like they were in their twenties. They had big blonde hair feathered back, spiked high-heeled shoes, skin-tight jeans, and low-cut shirts. I was stunned and I knew my parents would not let me out of the house looking that way. To top it off, I swear they had the biggest boobs I had ever seen on teenagers. I felt at that moment that I was out of my league. I was going to have to make some serious changes to fit in with this crowd, and I knew my parents were not going to go for the idea of me having a boob job so I had to find other ways.

I soon found that making these changes were going to be extremely difficult. My thick New York accent was the first thing that people heard and they teased me incessantly. Spanish class was a repetitive joke with my accent. I had to admit that saying the Spanish alphabet with my New York accent was humorous, but I learned to keep my mouth shut so I would not be constantly laughed at.

On Valentine's Day, students were selling singing telegrams to send to friends during class. A couple of boys sent me a singing telegram to the beat of "Short People Got No Reason." But they changed the lyrics so it said, "New Yorkers Got No Reason." The class went crazy laughing and cheering, and I laughed with them. Then I went home and cried my eyes out. I cried nearly every day after school that first year. I felt like I was different, ugly, and weird. I just did not feel like I fit in with the other kids. I longed to be back in New York with my life long friends and my sister.

On a positive note (well, at the time I thought it was positive...), I was thrilled to find out that drug use was rampant at my new school. It seemed everyone was partying on the weekends. Teenagers who have plenty of money never seem to lack drugs and alcohol. My parents did not have a clue I was drinking and drugging, and I kept my secret well-hidden from them. All my life they had taught me how to keep secrets and I was good at it. However, they questioned me when a story came out in one of the Texas magazines about drug-infested, suburban junior high schools. After seeing the article, they interrogated me about drugs at school. I told them the article was exaggerating (inside I was glad it was not) and I had never seen any kind of drugs ever. All they had to do was go upstairs and investigate my room. They would have found a baggie of pot and a bottle of Vodka I had swiped from them. I knew they never dreamed I would be doing anything of the sort.

Young drug abusers are up to three times more likely to suffer brain damage than those who do not use drugs. Damaged nerve cells are found in the areas of the brain involved in learning, memory and emotional well-being.[12]

My real reprieve came when I joined the city swim team. I had been swimming since the third grade, had broken many records and was awarded the Most Valuable Swimmer at my club in New York. I was ready to get in the pool again. It was a pleasant surprise to find many of the swimmers had also recently moved here from the east and we all felt like fish out of water at our new schools. I was also relieved when I found out many of them liked to party the way I did. The team became close extremely quickly. I now had some school friends and my swim team friends to party with. I began to think I might be able to survive this move after all. Friends, alcohol and drugs were going to be my saviors.

Reported illicit teen drug use: 8th grade 30.3%, 10th grade 44.9%, 12th grade 52.8%[13]

Even though I had been drinking for awhile, I remember my first experience at being exceedingly drunk. It was in Dallas and one of the swim team members was having a party at their house because their parents were not home. I recall bringing several bottles of the really sweet Boones Farm flavored wines. I did not realize that I drank nearly 3 bottles until I woke up from a blackout many hours later. This was my first experience with a blackout. During blackouts you function and usually no one else knows that you are in one. Of course, during blackouts you do things you would never do if you were sober.

I briefly remember making out in bed with one of the seniors on the team who I thought was really cute and then seeing a flash of light. Another guy from the team came in and took a picture of us in bed together. This was the last thing I remember before my memory got foggy. I do not know whatever happened to the picture or if I even had clothes on in the photo. All that I knew was that I had experienced my first black out and that drinking Boones Farm made me puke.

Chapter 5
Fear, Profanity & Reprieve

I was rarely home so I did not have to deal with my parents often. However, when I was home my father's dreadful raging did not stop. As his alcoholism continued to progress, his raging was evolving toward becoming more and more violent. For example, my mother had left a spoon in the sink and my father went off with his loud-mouth profanity. He started smashing dishes and throwing spoons, forks and knives around the kitchen.

I started to fear leaving my mother home alone with him because I was afraid he might hurt her. I tried talking to her about leaving him and encouraged her to get an apartment for us. I suggested going back to New York. I was old enough to realize that she did not have to live in that kind of abuse, and I could not fathom her continuing to live with him. I begged her to leave but she never would. I am convinced it would have been better to get a divorce in this kind of situation than stay with someone this sadistic. Not only would it better for the parents, but children should never have to endure this kind of cruelty and psychological abuse.

In the last thirty days, 50% of teenagers report drinking with 32% being drunk at least on one occasion.[14]

My dedicated codependent mother was too scared to leave my father; thus she stayed in the dysfunctional familiarity. Breaking out of the cycle of abuse is too overwhelmingly difficult for many to step out into the unfamiliar. My mother did not have the self-confidence or courage to do so. For decades all she had heard was how she was a miserable, stupid, piece of crap. Of course, she came to believe it. After my mother refused to leave, I was completely disgusted with her and lost all respect for her. At that young age, I just could not understand. I started to be sad all the time and would cry often over trivial mishaps. I had started showing signs of depression.

I was having more fun with guys and learning more about sex. Even though I was a virgin still, that didn't stop me from doing everything else. My self-confidence was lacking and I felt that boys would not be interested in me if I did not give them what they wanted. So I continually gave them what they wanted and it seemed to work. This eventually led to sex with my boyfriend Todd, who was a senior in at my school. We "dated" for over a year, which consisted of getting wasted and then having sex. I perceived that everyone else was doing the same thing. I was actually relieved to lose my virginity because so many girls were talking about having sex. I wanted to say that I had done it too. Just like drinking, I did not think there were any consequences to my sexual actions. Throughout high school, I never felt like I was good enough, pretty enough, smart enough or popular enough. I would do and try anything to feel differently, but I just kept sinking further into depression. I felt like I was only going through the motions of life, and it was tiresome.

Teens who drink are 50 times more likely to use cocaine than teens who never consumed alcohol.[15]

I got a break from my parents when I was 15 years-old and they started traveling. They started leaving me home alone while they went to the Virgin Islands and were gone for a week or two at a time. Their cars were in the garage and the liquor cabinet was stocked, so I took this to mean everything was free rein. Since I had little respect for my parents and absolutely no respect for myself, I did not think twice about taking advantage of the situation and abusing their property. I did not have my driver's license, but that did not stop me from driving my parent's cars all over Dallas. I usually felt like an outsider with the majority of kids at high school (except the swimmers). However when my parents went away, I would have massive parties at the house. This made me popular…at least briefly. I liked partying at home because I could smoke as much dope as I wanted and drink as much alcohol as I could. I knew that if I passed out, I was safe at home.

Research suggests that underage drinking accounts for up to 20% of all alcohol consumption in the United States.[16]

I had started dating different boys, and instead of meeting them somewhere, I broke my own rule and had them pick me up at the house. On one occasion, my sister was visiting and my date came into meet her. My father was in the bedroom and decided he would walk out in his underwear. I was so embarrassed my father was standing in his skivvies in the family room without a shirt. I rushed my date out the front door. My sister was shaken by my father's inappropriateness and confronted him. His actions did not shock me because I was accustomed to his absurdities. It had been along time since she had experienced how ridiculous his actions were.

Havoc seemed to be the norm at my house,and I often contributed to the problem. On one occasion when my parents were out of town, I had an afternoon party. It ended abruptly when they came home six hours earlier than I had expected.The house was a mess: curtains had been torn down; all the beds were unmade (because people had been utilizing the beds); a weekend's worth of beer bottles and pizza boxes were spread throughout the house and overflowed into the back yard; and a huge bong sat in the middle of the family room on the cocktail table.When my parents walked in there was a haze of pot smoke lingering and the aroma of stale alcohol floated throughout the entire house.

More than 60% of teens said that drugs were sold, used or kept at their school.[17]

I was grateful that all of my friends scattered out the nearest door or window before my father's boiling rage exploded. By now, I knew I could handle anything my father could dish out, but I could not bear to have my friends see how he acted. My father seethed with anger and after all the screaming and yelling subsided, I was only grounded for a brief time. I had them convinced that something like this had never happened before. I groveled and apologized until they believed me. Alcoholics are the best liars. I could convince anyone of anything if it benefited my agenda. Being a "Master Manipulator" was an art that I had acquired as my addiction disease progressed.

More than 4 in 10 who binge drink—had 5 or more drinks on the same occasion—in the past month used illegal drugs.[18]

Chapter 6
Disco Obliteration

During the summer before going into 11th grade, I started to regularly go to discos with Anna. The drinking age at that time was 18 years-old, and I had learned how to do my hair and make-up so I looked much older. My appearance had drastically changed and I looked like a Texas girl, not the little parochial school girl that I had once been. My favorite outfit was a slinky, spaghetti strapped top and electric blue, skin-tight, glittery disco pants. I felt like I looked like a million bucks and so did the older guys. Anna and I rarely paid to get into a club, we would hug on the doormen and give them a touchy and a feely and in we went. It was not a big feat for two pretty girls to get into a club, but I was impressed that I wasn't asked for ID. I also did not have to pay a cover charge. Once in the club, guys would buy most of our drinks. I loved being in the disco with the loud music. It blocked out everything in the outside world and I could concentrate on those big luscious fruity drinks. I would get obliterated drinking massive amounts of alcohol. We would then drive to Anna's and pass out.

Anna's curfew was later than mine so we spent the night at her house nearly every Friday and Saturday night so we could stay out later. The concept that we were drinking and driving and could wreck, killing ourselves or someone else, was lost on us. We thought we were invincible and drinking made us temporarily more confident.

An estimated total of 2,163,210 crashes in the United States involved alcohol. These crashes killed 16,792 and injured an estimated 513,000 people.[19]

I had my 17th birthday party at my favorite disco. Anna and I knew all the regulars there and it was quite a party. Drinks were endless and the blur of the evening became a whirlwind of music and alcohol. Earlier in the week, I had met a guy at the Country Club pool who was home from college for the summer. Jason was the most beautiful man I had ever seen. It was love at first sight for both of us. He joined us that night at the club for my party and we stayed together for nearly three years. Once again, alcohol, drugs and friends were my temporary saviors. Now Jason was included in the mix.

After meeting Jason, sex was no longer an occasional event. I felt like I was on cloud nine because we were in love and the sex was wonderful. He also introduced me to smoking hash. I would have preferred drinking, but I was with Jason and I would have done anything he wanted. However, one time after smoking hash one day with him, I started hallucinating. This was a completely different kind of high than I had ever experienced and it freaked me out. I did not like feeling that I did not have control of myself. It scared me and I made him promise he would never give anything like that to me again.

My friends on the swim team were a huge part of my saving grace. I would stay over at my friends Pam and Leslie's, who were sisters, on a regular basis so I didn't have to go home. I think their parents knew there was a problem at my home and were sympathetic. Pam and Leslie were not as wild as I was, but Leslie and I had our moments of crazy stupors together. Another close and special friend was Ryan; these three friends were some of the best friends that a person could ever desire. They were always there for me and I loved them dearly.

Swim practice was twice a day and we swam one to two hours in the morning and two to three hours in the afternoon. Many mornings some of my friends and I would smoke a joint at 5 am before practice and then go to school. At 3 pm we were released and would usually smoke another joint before afternoon practice. I joked that swimmers had to smoke dope to be stupid enough to keep our heads in the water for five or six hours a day. I thought no one in their right mind would volunteer to do that straight.

Even though I had close friends, I continued to feel that I was not good enough, smart enough, pretty enough or special enough. Though I hid it well from others, I lacked complete self-confidence in myself. I was miserable deep down and the only thing I found to relieve that deep dark pit of emptiness in my soul was drinking, drugging and sex. The problem was it was taking more alcohol and drugs to suppress all my hideous feelings.

Compared with men, women with drinking problems have an increased risk for depression, low self-esteem, alcohol-related physical problems, marital discord or divorce, spouses with alcohol problems, a history of sexual abuse, and drinking in response to life crises.[20]

Chapter 7
Depressed and Dejected

This is about the time my depression became serious. I was not motivated to do anything and I cried constantly. A teenager suffering from depression is common when they have lived in a dysfunctional and abusive home for so long. Added to the family dysfunction was my drinking and drugging. This combination made for one dejected and very unhappy kid. After years of hearing my father scream that I was dumb, stupid and useless, all the anger I had turned inward had now turned into depression. I did not know at the time depression would be something I would battle for many years. My mother took me to the doctor and he put me on some medication for depression. The medicine did not help, but I liked it because it gave me a great buzz. However, I was taken off the drug when I accidentally set my science experiment on fire in lab and then I skipped down the hall singing. The Principal did not find this as humorous as my friends and I did, but there were not any serious consequences.

Swim meets were often in other cities and they turned into bashes with alcohol and drugs in our hotel rooms. I looked forward to these meets, but I was not concentrating on improving my times. I was anxious to party hard with my friends and that was all I cared about. One of my swimming friends had been telling me about quaaludes and how if you took one you would get a buzz like you had drunk a dozen beers. This sounded fantastic because I often puked from drinking too much. So I experimented with quaaludes and then went for a drive in my car with some other kids. Well, they were right, the pill made me feel really drunk and no matter how hard I tried, I could not keep the car in the lane. I thought that quaaludes were heaven sent and I would never have another hangover again!

In 2002, about 11 million persons aged 12 or older reported driving under the influence of illegal drugs during the past year. That is, 31% of illicit drug users were under the influence of illegal drugs while driving at least once in the past year.[21]

Quaaludes became a new friend, but I still was not willing to let go of my old comforting friend...alcohol. Besides, quaaludes were more difficult to come by and alcohol was everywhere. I sometimes would do both because the combination would get me higher than using them solo. All of my insecurities and emptiness vanished instantly, and there was a wonderful warm feeling of oblivion. When I was in that state of mind and high as a kite, no one was there to judge me and I was not coherent enough to judge myself. I longed for that unconsciousness.

Right before my senior year, I hurt my shoulder badly and I was in excruciating pain. I was not able to swim and all my goals as an athlete faded away. This added to my depression and gave me more of a reason to continue on my alcoholic demise.

I went to clubs at least three days a week and on the weekends would visit Jason at college in San Marcos. I only needed a few classes to graduate so I did not take my senior year seriously. My grades were always good, but I kept skipping school. Once, two of my friends and I decided we would go to "Happy Hour" for cheap margaritas. By 10 am, we were sitting at a Mexican restaurant's bar waiting to order our frozen delights. None of us had eaten and it never crossed our minds that we should. By 4 pm in the afternoon, we were still sitting at the bar drinking ourselves into near unconsciousness. They took me home around 5 pm and I was so drunk that I could not walk into the house. My mother had to come out and practically carry me. I made it into the house and I immediately started puking. I knew I could not lie my way out of this one, so I told her the truth. It was probably the first time in my life I had tried this tactic.

Alcohol kills 6½% times more teenagers than all other illicit drugs combined.[22]

The next three days were a big blur. I had never been so physically ill in my life. My mother took me to the emergency room because I could not stop dry heaving and puking. We found out I had a severe case of alcohol poisoning. My alcohol level was so high the doctor said he could not believe I was still coherent. He stressed I was lucky to be alive. I did not get out of bed and could barely function for nearly a week. I thought I was going to die and the idea did not seem like a bad option. My mother never told my father what was really wrong with me and saved us both from one of his colossal rage attacks.

The death rate among women alcoholics is higher than among males because of their increased risk for suicide, alcohol-related accidents, cirrhosis and hepatitis.[23]

Chapter 8
Seized By the Disease

"Teenagers whose parents talk to them regularly about the dangers of drugs are 42% less likely to use drugs than those whose parents don't, yet only 1 in 4 teens reports having those conversations." [24]

After the alcohol poisoning, I swore I had learned my lesson. I would never drink again. That oath lasted about three weeks and I was off on a roll again drinking as much as ever.

Nearly every weekend I would fly down to stay with Jason at college. I told my parents I was staying with a girlfriend at the dorm and they never questioned it. I was still head-over-heels in love with Jason. He was gorgeous and popular. He also thought I was beautiful and always wanted to party. We were a match made in heaven, so I thought. Jason sometimes sold drugs to support himself through college. This never bothered me because I rationalized to myself it showed signs of creativity and entrepreneurship. It did not matter if he would have been a convicted felon ten times over, I would have rationalized that too. We loved each other and that was all that mattered. His having easy access to drugs just solidified the deal.

My mother was getting upset with me because I kept skipping school. My favorite trick was to skip on Mondays because I stayed Saturday and Sunday in San Marcos. Thus I had a three day weekend. One Friday she told me that I could go to San Marcos, but I had to be home Sunday evening and be in school on Monday. She was tired of my lame excuses for missing school and was getting angry at me. The weekend came and went. It was about 10 pm on Sunday evening and I was still in San Marcos. I had missed all the flights home and I called and told her. I had never heard her as furious as she was that night and I knew I was in hot water. I was used to hearing my father that way, but not my mother.

She knew Jason's friend, David, was in San Marcos that weekend. She told me to get a ride home with David. I explained it was not a good idea for me to ride back with him and tried hinting to her that David would have drugs in the car. However, she told me she did not care what was in the car. I was to leave immediately and get home before school in the morning. I explained I was seriously concerned about getting arrested if I rode with him. She did not care because she had taken enough crap from me, and she probably thought it was another tired lie.

The increase in the use of marijuana has been especially pronounced. Between 1992 and 2005 past-month use of marijuana increased from: 12% to 20% among high school seniors, 8% to 15% among 10th graders and 4% to 7% among 8th graders.[25]

I knew she meant business, but I also knew riding with David could be a disaster. David drove a gold Trans Am with a huge bird on the hood, tinted windows, and big tires with matching gold rims. As if that was not enough to be a cop magnet, the license plates were from New York and expired. It was impossible to be inconspicuous in a car like that. It might as well have had a flashing red light on top alerting the cops to pull us over. Being pulled over was a major concern because he was carrying three large trash bags full of dope in the trunk and a bag of cocaine in the glove compartment; I knew we were destined for jail.

David and I left San Marcos at midnight and arrived in Dallas around 4 am. We started the trip tired and bored but that did not last long. He showed me how to snort a few bumps of cocaine and instantly we were wide awake. This was the first time I remember doing coke and I knew from the very first rail I had found my next addiction. After only a rail or two, I felt I was on top of the world and in complete control. We talked non-stop having weird intense conversations all the way back to Dallas. David gave me a little coke to take with me so that I would not be too tired for school. My mother never asked any questions about how I had gotten home and I never volunteered the information. I was amazed and grateful we had not been pulled over. There was only one word to describe our avoiding getting busted…lucky.

Up to 75% of people who try cocaine will become addicted to it. Only one out of four people who try to quit will be able to do so without help.[26]

After my little episode with David, I decided not to go and visit Jason for awhile. My father was not accustomed to having me around the house, and I do not think he was as pleased as my mother was about it. I was waiting for the ball to drop and one day it did. Unbeknownst to me, my garage door opener accidentally fell out of my car in the driveway. When my father found it, he went into a horrific rage and started his usual boisterous screaming. However, this time his rage escalated further than I had ever seen. He could not stop yelling and he was shaking uncontrollably with anger. I did not know what he was going to do so I ran upstairs to my room, slammed my door shut and locked it as fast as I could. He ran after me and broke my door down to get to me. He then hit me for the very first time in my life. His rage had spiraled out of control and he was not just emotionally abusive anymore. Now he was physical.

Alcohol is present in more than one-half of all incidents of domestic violence.[27]

After he left, I just laid in bed for hours, thinking that life was not worth living anymore. I could not handle the immense emotional pain that gored me inside. I thought physical pain would be much easier to endure. My insides were bleeding with the guilt and remorse of everything I had turned into and knew my father hated me. At seventeen years-old, I was a full-blown alcoholic and addict with severe depression and complete lack of self-esteem. In other words, I felt worthless and hopeless.

At the time, I did not realize that while my father's disease of alcoholism had progressed, mine had also. The worst part was that I was turning into him and I could not see it. I had the same kind of rage, but I was keeping it locked away inside. Thus, it was manifesting as depression. My outward rage had not started yet.

Chapter 9
Graduation Desperation

Graduation was just around the corner and I was thrilled. This meant only one summer left at home. Jason would be back in Dallas soon and I relied on him (instead of myself) to make me feel better again. It was only a few short months until I was at college with him. So I continued to bury my depression and guilt deep down inside. It was easy not expressing my true feelings, I had not done this all my life. It was the only way I knew how to survive. I was scared to actually feel anything…it was easier to ignore it.

Binge drinking and heavy drinking are highest among 18 to 25 years old.[28]

I could not get out of high school fast enough. Graduation was a relief to me and the "Class of 1981" had a huge party in a barn way out in the boonies. Everyone seemed to be there and if you were going to gauge having a good time by the amount of alcohol ingested, then my friends and I had a hellacious time.

It was early into the next morning and people started to head home. Once again, the dangers of drinking and driving never crossed our minds. It's the old, "It will never happen to me syndrome." A friend was with me and I was driving. I could hardly see the country road for the lack of street lights and the amount of alcohol in my system. I was driving slowly when I noticed that one of the cars in front of me seemed to disappear. As I came up on the spot, I noticed that my friend's car had gone straight through a road barrier. It did not even look like a car anymore. It was demolished the classmates who were on the scene said that two of my classmates died on impact. However, one was still alive. It took a while for an ambulance to get there. When they finally did, it was not hopeful that my other friend would last very long. He did not.

In 2004, 30% of all fatal crashes were alcohol-related, compared to 51% on weekends.[29]

The entire evening felt like an episode from *The Twilight Zone*. It started with such a joyous, wonderful occasion and ended up with two dead friends and another bleeding to death. I prayed I would wake up from the nightmare, but I did not.

Most people who had three classmates die in a drunk driving accident on graduation night would take heed to the lesson. But I completely ignored what had happened. This way I did not have to deal with the reality of the seriousness of my drinking and drugging problems.

For fatal crashes occurring from midnight to 3:00 am, 77% involved alcohol in 2003.[30]

August and my 18th birthday came quickly, and I was ready to start a new life at college with Jason. The problem with that theory was the old saying, "wherever you go, there you are" held true. In other words, the resentments, negative feelings, depression and rage were still buried inside of me and blasting out inappropriately at different intervals. Nothing about how I felt changed just because I was in a different city away from my parents. It was never an option whether I was going to college in my family. We all went right after high school. At the time, I did not appreciate I was getting an education. All I knew was if I kept my grades up then my parents would pay for everything and I had a free ride to party for four years.

My mother and my sister encouraged me to go through rush and join a sorority. It seemed really odd to me these girls were standing in circles, holding hands and singing, but I thought it would be something different and it might be good for me. I went through the motions of the traditions and pledging because I was meeting some incredible friends. I was also looking forward to the parties and the formals because I knew they would involve alcohol.

As many as 360,000 of the nation's 12 million undergraduates will ultimately die from alcohol-related causes. This is more than the number who will be awarded advanced degrees.[31]

Jason's fraternity Little Sisters decided to adopt me and I was included in a party at one of their apartments. I thought I was so grown-up and mature because I was going to an older girl's apartment while I was a freshman living in the dorm. The Little Sisters played a drinking game called "Quarters" for hours. You had to bounce a quarter on the table into a beer and if the quarter missed then you had to drink the beer. If you bounced the quarter and it went into the beer then you chose who drank next. The game continued around the table all night. I could not get a quarter to bounce into a mug of beer if my life had depended on it. So, I ended up getting drunker than I ever imagined.

Nearly 4 million American women ages 18 and older can be classified as alcoholic or problem drinkers, one-third the number of men; of these women, 58% are between the ages of 18 to 29.[32]

The next thing I remember is waking up at Jason's the next morning. He was livid because I had passed out naked in the middle of his living room and he had roommates. Having his roommates see me naked was the last thing on my mind. My head was dizzy, my stomach was churning and all I could do was puke. I tried lying on the bed with one foot off to stop the room from spinning but it was useless. I was beyond the point of being ill so I went to the doctor at the campus infirmary. He confirmed my suspicions, I had alcohol poisoning...again. The doctor lectured me that I was lucky to still be breathing and it was going to be awhile before I felt any better. I threw up my guts up for days and, after about a week, I started to at least function somewhat like a human being again.

Alcohol poisoning cost the United States $500,000,000 in 2005.[33]

I could not understand how I had drunk so much to get alcohol poisoning again. When I had gotten so ill in high school, I had sworn never to drink that much again. This time it was worse and I was disgusted with myself. Once I sobered up, I started wondering how many of Jason's friends had seen me lying naked on the living room floor.

The disgust I had for myself was promptly forgotten by the time the next party arrived. Once again, I was with the fraternity's Little Sisters and we went to buy some wine and beer. I went into the store and bought what we needed while they waited in the car. As I was leaving the store, a policeman approached and stopped me. He asked me for my driver's license. On September first of that year, the drinking age changed to 21 years-old and I was only 18. I had just purchased alcohol without even thinking twice about it. I had been buying alcohol since I was 15 and it was a regular part of my weekend activities. It had never occurred to me I was breaking the law and could be arrested.

Students who binge drink are more likely to vandalize property, have unprotected sex, poor academic performance, and participate in a sexual assault.[34]

The most ridiculous part of the entire situation was the Little Sisters waiting in the car were 21 years-old and could have legally bought the alcohol. The officer was kind and did not arrest me. Instead, he wrote me a ticket for buying alcohol when I was underage. I knew I had barely scraped by this time and I believe now I was not arrested because I was a cute college female freshman. My looks had gotten me out of a lot of hassles in the past and I was grateful they had come through again.

When I told my parents about the ticket they laughed and told me to be more careful. I sent the ticket home, they paid it and I learned absolutely nothing from that experience. However, the first semester, I did learn three very valuable lessons. *First*, eat before I drink. Drinking on an empty stomach made me puke. *Second*, don't smoke dope and drink at the same time. It made my head swirl and then I would puke. Pick one or the other but not both. *Third*, remember that the drinking age is 21 and that I am not suppose to buy alcohol. I am sure my parents would have been elated to know their money was being well spent on such a wonderful education.

In 2003, a total of 20,687 persons died of alcohol-induced causes in the United States. This includes not only deaths from dependent and independent use of alcohol, but also accidental poisoning by alcohol.[35]

Chapter 10
Addicts Will Be Addicts

During college, I thought all the partying I was doing was great, and I also thought I was having a blast. Figuring out how not to puke every time I drank became a chemistry experiment for me. One solution I tried was not to drink every night and that seemed to help a lot. Besides, if I drank every day then that meant I could have a drinking problem. Even though I was not drinking daily, I had already progressed past the binge drinking stage and was headed straight to full blown alcoholism. I was in denial and did not have an inkling about the havoc my disease was and would continue to have on me and the people around me.

43% of college students say they are binge drinkers and 21% say they binge frequently Binge drinking is defined as consuming five or more drinks in a row at one sitting for boys and four or more for girls.[36]

My grades were alright, but they were nothing near what I was capable of making. The only reason I bothered studying and keeping my grades up was I knew if I flunked then I would have to go back home to the dysfunction. I was determined not to let that happen. My priorities included drinking/drugging, Jason, going to class and studying-all in that order. I thought I was in heaven and I was having the time of my life. There were no more episodes of my father's raging and I did not have to walk on egg shells all the time. I felt I was finally free from my dysfunctional home life. However, I was oblivious to the real situation I was following in my father's foot steps of alcoholism and soon the feelings I had stuffed for so many years would start to explode into rage. I was ignorant to the facts; I was becoming exactly what I despised.

More than half of all adults have a family history of alcoholism or problem drinking.[37]

There was a local club where college students hung out all the time and I went there often. They sold quarter drinks and the drinks were made of cheap, bottom of the barrel, rock gut liquor. A group of us were talking about a girl who had left the club the week before and so intoxicated that she got on the highway going the wrong way and drove head-on into traffic. She hit an eighteen wheeler and had been killed instantly. As we were talking about what happened, we continued to drink our cheap booze knowing that we were all going to drive home. The club had installed a breathalyzer machine so patrons could blow into it before they left. Jokingly, my friends were blowing into the machine to see what their alcohol content showed. I blew into the machine and it read that I was in a coma. I had so much alcohol in my system that it was off the charts. We all laughed hysterically and I rationalized that the machine was messed up and the reading was wrong. I then drove home in a drunken, coma-induced state-of- mind.

Every year, 1,400 American college students between the ages of 18 and 24 die from inadvertent alcohol-related injuries, including motor vehicle accidents.[38]

Late one night, I was "kidnapped" by Jason's fraternity and asked to become a Little Sister. I wanted this more than anything and I was so excited. I thought that once I was a Little Sister I would be part of the "in crowd." This was something I never felt in high school. I also knew being a Little Sister would open doors to being included in more parties and even being a hostess. I had the notion being in a fraternity would be much more fun than being in a sorority because my fraternity was a group of guys and the Little Sisters who drank and partied relentlessly. Not only did they drink like I did, but they sincerely cared about me and treated me like I was their real little sister. I honestly loved how wonderful and special they made me feel. I would have done anything for any of them. The drinking was just an extra added bonus.

80% of college students drink and 48% of these students feel drinking to get drunk is an important reason to drink.[39]

It's difficult to try to describe the fraternity parties. To say they were rowdy and undisciplined would be an understatement. The parties were always getting out of hand and something would always get wrecked in the house. So the logical solution was to move all the furniture out into the front yard. Nothing got broken after that (except the windows) and we ended up with some great yard furniture. I felt like I was living in the movie *Animal House*, and I fit right in with all the crazy lunatics.

Fraternity and sorority members drink more alcohol and more frequently than their peers. They also accept as normal drinking high levels of alcohol consumption and associated problems as normal.[40]

There were some outrageous stunts pulled at the parties. One drunk dude jumped from the second floor balcony onto the fraternity letters propped up against the house and slid down. Thankfully, drunks seem to be made of rubber and nothing was broken.

Sometimes, when the fraternity house got too bizarre, we would go to a brother's trailer house to party in a smaller crowd. The trailer was appropriately nicknamed "The Shack" because that's just about what the trailer looked like. "The Shack" had a room where everyone would sit on the floor in a circle. A string hung from the ceiling with a roach clip attached and it was always in the center of the circle. We would light a joint, snap it on the roach clip and then fling the string and the lighted joint to someone across the circle. It probably would have made better sense to pass to the person next to you, but that would have taken the fun out of trying to catch a lit joint that was just hurled at you.

Each year, college students spend $5.5 billion on alcohol (mostly beer). This is more than they spend on books, soda, coffee, juice and milk combined.[41]

I was already wasted before joining in the circle. When the joint was thrown at me, I missed it and it hit me in the forehead. I finally caught it and took a few drags. I then chucked it back across the circle. Jason then realized that something smelled funny (not the joint). He looked at me and discovered my hair was on fire. He quickly grabbed a beer and poured it on my head. We were so stoned that all we could do was laugh. Later that evening, when I looked in the mirror I saw that my bangs were completely burned off. They were gone and I looked ridiculous. I had no idea what I was going to tell people. A revelation occurred to me. I could have burned my face or been hit in the eye with the flying joint. But it was just a flickering revelation, because just as fast as it went into my brain, it went right out.

The number of young people using illegal drugs peaks in the 18–20 year age range with 22 in 100 using illegal drugs in the past month.[42]

Chapter 11
Rage-a-holic

Looking back, it was obvious that I was in full blown alcoholism and drug addiction when I was a freshman, although I was completely unaware of it. All I cared about was not flunking out, and where my next drink and drug were coming from. The fraternity bashes were unbelievable, and they never ceased to amuse me. Many times the fraternities on campus would have huge trash cans full of some kind of concoction appropriately named "Trash Can Punch." It usually consisted of whatever liquor was on sale at the store, what was left around the house and what people brought to the party. Then a red fruit punch would be mixed with everything and wha-la! - you would have the infamous "Trash Can Punch." I found out first hand the problem with the punch was it was really sweet, so you could not taste the alcohol. Girls were usually the ones drinking the punch, and they would get wasted exceedingly fast because they could not taste the liquor. The red punch tasted grotesque, but I would drink it anyway. Often after drinking it, I would puke and it looked like I was puking blood all over the place. This was my idea of college fun.

Research suggests that women may be at higher risk for developing alcohol-related problems at lower levels of consumption than men.[43]

I stopped drinking the punch after one of the parties when some jerk threw hits of acid into the punch. I had no idea that the "Trash Can Punch" had turned into "Acid Punch" and I went into a complete blackout. I have no idea what happened past 10 pm that evening. I never drank the punch again. I hated feeling out of control and having blackouts when I drank too much. Cocaine gave me the false sense of being in complete control and is the sensation that I thrived on.

The feeling of not being in control is what convinced me I needed to lay off of my drinking and stick with cocaine. It was the 80s and cocaine was rampant and easily accessible...especially if you were a pretty young college girl. I rarely paid for cocaine because my friends would always have it or were selling it. I just made sure the guys I hung out with or dated had the right connections and a supply.

70% of AIDS cases among women are drug related.[44]

Jason and I dated for nearly three years and I loved him. However, it was time for a change. Instead of taking a break from each other, we completely split up, and I told him I never wanted to see him again. The unreasonable characteristics of alcoholism were prevalent. Everything had to be taken to the extreme. It had to either be black or white; there was no grey area. After three years, our relationship was completely over in a flash; it was all or nothing.

Since I despised myself, I could not be alone or without a boyfriend for very long. The longer a person is alone they eventually have to take the time to look at themselves. When there is someone else in your life, then you can focus all your energies on them. You never have to look within yourself. Even though my father was not around on a daily basis I was still feeling empty, unworthy and unlikable. A geographic cure for my addictions was not working very well- "where ever you go there you are." I was definitely in worse shape than ever, with a progressive disease consuming my thoughts and actions from the inside out.

400,000 students between the ages of 18 and 24 have had unprotected sex, and more than 100,000 students between the ages of 18 and 24 report having been too intoxicated to know if they consented to having sex.[45]

I immediately found a new boyfriend named Bobby. He was blonde, blue-eyed, gorgeous, and very tall. He also had a vastly different personality than Jason. He belonged to the "Pretty Boy" fraternity on campus, and rightfully so. I met Bobby during Homecoming week and that, of course, included partying heavily. I would have never dated anyone who did not have the same partying habits, and Bobby's idea of partying was the same as mine.

College students drink an estimated 4 billion cans of beer each year. The total amount of alcohol consumed by them annually is 430 million gallons, which is enough for each college and university in the United States to fill an Olympic size pool.[46]

Bobby used cocaine more than I had been accustomed and it was a fabulous surprise for an addict whose drug of choice was coke. We hit it off immediately. We were fresh and different for each other and the newness novelty did not wear off quickly. The sex was sensational. We would do coke for hours upon hours and then stay up all night and have sex. We would sleep far into the afternoon on the weekends and then get up and study so we could stay in school.

Cocaine is the second most commonly used illicit drug (following marijuana) in the United States. More than 34 million Americans (14.7%) age 12 or older have used cocaine at least once in their lifetime.[47]

I pretended to be the good girl and act like I did not have the "recreational habits" I did so I would not get in trouble with my sorority. However, there were some sorority sisters who drank and drugged just like me so we stuck together. Even though I was a great liar, with as many drugs as I was doing, I was having difficulties keeping up with all my lies and cover-ups. It seemed like everything was slowly catching up to me. But if anything did surface, I would just lie my way out of that too.

Since I was already far into my alcoholism and drug addiction, Bobby was exposed to my irrational behaviors immediately. Bobby was one of the sweetest, gentlest men I had ever met and we loved each other genuinely. When we were not drinking and using drugs, we would have an extraordinary time together. We had the same interests and sense of humor, and we would laugh and play around time and again. But when we were partying, we were destined for trouble. We would have horrific fights, and I started going into rages. Then I would black out. My rages began happening more frequently. They scared me because all I could think about was how my father acted. I hated having raging fits and I felt more and more guilt every time. I knew that something was wrong with me, but I did not know what to do about it. I was afraid if I asked for help someone would tell me I was crazy and I would be locked away in an asylum. My rages were embarrassing and I did not want anyone knowing the extent of them. However, Bobby knew them all too well.

80% of students who live on college campuses who do not binge drink report that they have experienced at least one second-hand effect of binge drinking, such as being the victim

of an assault or an unwanted sexual advance, having property vandalized or having sleep or study interrupted.[48]

One evening, after doing our partying rituals, Bobby and I got into another fight. I drove to his house and I ran in to the meat freezer in the laundry room. I was screaming, yelling, cussing, and threatening him. Unbeknownst to me, because I was in a blackout, I took the meat out of the freezer and started hitting myself in the head with it and then throwing it at him. Eventually, Bobby was able to stop me and hold me down until I calmed down. I sobbed until I fell asleep in his arms.

Almost 700,000 college students between the ages of 18 and 24 are assaulted by another student who has been drinking.[49]

Chapter 12
Ill-conceived Fantasy

My friend Alexis and I began hanging out with each other a great deal. We had the same lifestyle and became very close. We always seemed to have plenty of money for whatever we wanted, which was usually coke. One night when we had driven to Austin, and we were sitting in my yellow Mustang (my high school graduation gift). It was dark outside and we did not hesitate to take out our mirrors and rail out a few lines of coke. We were in the middle of indulging ourselves when we heard cheering and clapping. We looked up through my sunroof and there was a crowd of people standing on the balcony directly above my car watching us. They loved witnessing a private illegal moment between two lovely young women and when we got out of our car they invited us up to their party. We declined knowing that they just wanted some of our precious cocaine and we were not about to share it with a bunch of strangers.

All of my friends and I had been living for so many years thinking we were invincible and nothing would ever happen to us. We thought we would not get arrested for drunk driving and we never thought about wrecking a car, killing ourselves or worse killing someone else and living. We lived our lives like we were indestructible.

2.1 million students between the ages of 18 and 24 drove under the influence of alcohol in 2002.[50]

We were all rudely awakened from this ill-conceived fantasy with a tragedy that devastated all my fraternity brothers and sisters. Two of my Little Sister friends, Charlotte and Tina, decided to go to Austin for a trip down 6th Street. Charlotte drove her glorious hot rod...a new sports car. Another friend went along. Because there were three people in a two seater car, their friend sat in the middle. Tina was in the passenger's seat and Charlotte was driving. In a drunken state of mind, Charlotte crashed the car Tina and the other passenger were killed. Charlotte survived the accident physically, but mentally she would have to live the rest of her life knowing she had just killed two people. Tina and Charlotte had been best friends and to have their friendship end this way was unfathomable.

Almost half of all traffic fatalities are alcohol related.[51]

Both friends who died in the sports car that evening had been drinking just as heavily as Charlotte. They were aware that they were risking their safety by getting in the car with her. I believe they are just as responsible for what occurred as Charlotte. If I choose to get into a car with someone who has been drinking, then I am putting myself at risk and I am just as much responsible for anything that may happen as the driver. I can not conceive how someone could cope with life after such a staggering catastrophe, but many do.

28.5% of college students who during the past 30 days rode in a vehicle 1 or more times with a driver who had been drinking alcohol.[52]

All of my fraternity brothers and sisters were heartbroken over the disaster. We realized we were not as invincible as we had led ourselves to believe. We were jolted into a very sad reality.

I recalled that less than three years earlier, I experienced my three drunken high school classmates death on graduation night. I had conveniently overlooked this memory until the same scenario happened again. Then it all came rushing back and I could not help but think about both disasters and what a waste of precious lives the accidents had been. All I could keep thinking were these tragedies could have happened to nearly everyone I knew, including myself.

I had it ingrained in my heart and soul that I was never going to drink and drive again. In reality, there were very few times after going out during college, where I was sober enough to be driving. Even though my friends were dying in wrecks, I still would not relent that it could happen to me. But inevitably driving drunk will catch up to you and it finally did for me.

My fraternity brother Aaron and I were in Dallas for the summer and we went back to San Marcos for a summer fraternity reunion. We flew into Austin where Aaron rented a car and off we went to party for the weekend with our brothers and sisters. We had been drinking at the fraternity house for awhile when we decided we would go to Austin. It never failed, drinks on 6th Street were endless and we were exceedingly wasted. It was time to head home before one of us, or both of us passed out or got arrested.

Aaron and I headed back to my college apartment, but somehow we ended up driving around in an area of San Marcos with narrow, hilly, curvy roads and huge old trees. Next thing I knew, I was driving and telling

Aaron that I wanted to be a race car driver. I had just woken up from a blackout and realized we were whizzing around winding roads going foolishly fast. It was just a matter of a few minutes when I lost control of the car and crashed head on into a huge tree going approximately 50 mph.

In 2004, between the ages of 16–24 years old, 14% were involved in alcohol related fatal crashes.[53]

When I woke up I was lying on top of Aaron on a gravel road and I was in shock. I could not believe I had just totaled a car and nearly killed both of us. The car looked like a piece of tin foil that had been crumbled. The driver's seat was completely annihilated and was no longer there. The steering wheel was mashed into the front seat and the roof on the driver's side was completely smooshed down into the seat…exactly where I had been sitting. Somehow before we crashed Aaron had grabbed me and pulled me out his door and we rolled in the gravel. We were not wearing our seatbelts and our doors were not locked. If they had been, we could both have died. It was unusual that I did not have my seat belt on and I usually locked the doors, but this time they were not. Later I would realize that God and our Guardian Angels were with us both that night protecting us.

We stood there staring at the car in amazement, not knowing what to do. A police car pulled up to the scene and when the officer got out of the car, he knew exactly who I was. He was one of my school instructors. He looked at me and told me to start walking away and leave immediately. He said he would come by my apartment later and talk to me. Aaron and I started walking until we found the closest phone. I knew I had to call my parents, so I bit the bullet and called them. By now the accident had caused a "quick sobering up" and I was somewhat coherent. I told my father what had happened (leaving out the drugs and alcohol) knowing I was far enough away from him that he could not hurt me. Furthermore, I could hang up if he blew his stack. To my surprise, he was very calm and was actually concerned. He asked if either of us were hurt and if we needed to go to the hospital. I told him we were all right and he sounded relieved. My father told me to go to my apartment and wait for the police officer. That is exactly what we did.

A new study shows that 6% of college students meet the criteria for a diagnosis of alcohol dependence (referred to as alcoholism) and 31% meet the clinical criteria for alcohol abuse.[54]

I could not believe that my father actually cared about me. I had no idea that he would not be upset, but concerned. It was a drastic encounter to experience when realizing that my father actually cared, but at least I had found out. I was grateful that I had caught him when he was not in a drunken haze.

Aaron's father was a Dallas police officer. Calling him and telling him I had just totaled his son's rented car was not a pleasant experience. However, Aaron and I made it through the phone calls and caught a ride back to my apartment. When news spread that we had been in a wreck some of my fraternity brothers came over to check on us. My head hurt, because I hit it somehow when I fell out of the car. I should have gone to the hospital, but I rationalized if I had a concussion the doctors would simply tell me to stay awake for awhile, so I did. My kind- hearted fraternity brothers brought cocaine over and I snorted rails all night. I figured if I had a concussion the coke would keep me from falling asleep and I would be alright. While we were snorting, the police officer knocked on my door. We quickly hid the coke, let him in and he gave me a ticket for reckless driving. Once again, I believe being a cute little college girl got me off the hook, and I did not get in the kind of trouble I should have.

Many of my friends were very upset about the accident. After losing Tina just a short time before, they did not know how I could be so irresponsible. They could not believe I had been stupid enough to almost have killed Aaron and myself. They were right and I knew it. At least some of my partying friends understood the reality of drunk driving. I wish I could say that was the last time that I drank and drove, but it was not.

Chapter 13
X: The Intense Bliss

Bobby and I had been dating for awhile and living a lifestyle that never seemed to slow down. The next step in our relationship was to get engaged so we did. I was happy to be marrying Bobby, but underneath that happiness were all my feelings of depression, rage, suicidal tendencies and sadness. I was an alcoholic and an addict progressing rapidly with her disease. Our relationship did not have a chance of making it from the very start because my inner-self was in a disarray of turmoil.

Approximately 35.3 million Americans aged 12 and older have tried cocaine at least once in their life times, representing 14.3% of the population.[55]

Ecstasy also known as X was a new drug that became very popular on campus and, at the time, it was legal. It was a lot cheaper than coke and many people were saying that the high was an intense bliss. I was told when you took X you would love everyone and anyone around. It was explained a person's worst enemy could walk in the room and you would tell them you loved them and then give them a big hug and kiss. There was no way I was going to pass up trying this new "miracle" drug. Once again my rationalizing skills were utilized and I figured, since it was legal, there could not be any harm involved.

There were 977,000 persons aged 12 and older who had used cocaine for the first time in the last 12 months. This averages to approximately 2,700 new users a day.[56]

X was everything and more than I had heard. The exhilaration of happiness I felt was so intense. It was no surprise they called the drug Ecstasy. The first time I took it Bobby and I sat with each other all night at a club laughing and touching each other because we were experiencing a new high I had never thought possible. Sex that evening was the most intense erotic sex we had ever had. X makes all your senses more heightened with incredible elated sensations.

Ecstasy was a drug categorized as a "Designer Drug." It sold for about $10-$20 a pill compared to about $150 for a gram of coke. The drugs popularity skyrocketed almost over night and it became the new instant phenomenon. X was not grown from a plant like pot or cocaine. Instead, X was usually made in some guy's bathtub with a concoction of a variety of drugs. So sometimes when you would get an X, it would be pink and sometimes blue and sometimes yellow and sometimes white with pink dots. I did not ever know what I was taking. My girl friends and I would joke that we were going to have babies with three heads, as we downed our X. Future consequences were thrown out the window.

***Percentage of 12th grade students who had tried Ecstasy at least once in 2003, 12.8% and in 2005, 5.4%*[57]**

I started to lose a lot of weight. I was already overly thin and when I started to lose weight it was very noticeable. I had not been feeling very well and could not eat or drink very much because I would throw up or have diarrhea. After about a week of puking blood and having bloody diarrhea, Bobby took me to the doctor. The doctor took one look at me and said I was completely dehydrated and malnutritioned. I was admitted to the hospital within an hour.

I was diagnosed with a parasite in my intestine called Giardia. The parasite is sometimes found in the Colorado River and can be deadly. I was put in isolation (it was highly contagious) and I had a continuous flow of blood coming out of both ends. My mother came and sat with Bobby. Together they watched me lay there in misery. I was informed that the lady in isolation before me had the same parasite and had died…not very encouraging.

The doctor never questioned my drinking or drug habits. I probably did not have any drugs left in my system because by the time I went to the hospital I had been sick for awhile. My body had time to detoxify itself. However, I knew if I had not been partying the way I was I would not have been as ill as I was. Between the parasite, the alcohol and the drugs, I had almost killed myself.

***For 2005, hospital emergency department mentions were estimated at 10,752 for Ecstasy use.*[58]**

I was in the hospital for quite a while and had to be released in time to take my GMAT, a test to get into graduate school. Even if I was high, I had found time to study for tests. However, I had not studied enough for the GMAT. I did not have a chance of getting a good score when I went into take the test. I was released from the hospital on Friday and on Saturday morning I was taking a day-long graduate-level test. I could not focus because of the medicine and I could barely stay awake. Needless to say, I did not do well on the test. Before the results came back from the test, I went to the head of the graduate program and explained what had happened. Of course, I omitted the part about the alcohol and drug abuse. He accepted me on a probationary status based on recommendations from my professors.

After the hospital experience, Bobby and I decided we needed some rest and relaxation away from college. So within a week of getting out of the hospital, I was on a plane with Bobby going to Cozumel, Mexico. Although I was barely able to keep liquids and food down and I had just stopped bleeding from both ends, we were on our way to Mexico.

We relaxed and laid on the crystal clear ocean and sandy white beach. The sun was a lot more intense than what we were accustomed to in Texas and we were sun burned badly. Therefore, we sat several days under the thatched huts and watched the blue waves drift into the shore. I had promised my mother that I would not drink any alcohol because of the medicine that I was taking. I really intended not to drink anything, but my alcoholism taunted me. I had to try a frozen fruity drink with cherry, pineapple and a darling little umbrella. One lead to several, and Bobby and I were off on another drinking spree. Even just being released from the hospital and being near death did not stop me from drinking again. Alcohol was a part of me like breathing. It was a necessity to life. Drinking was my norm so it did not feel like I was doing something wrong. It was just what I had always done and I never considered stopping as a real option.

We came back from our trip and began celebrating like we always did. Bobby and I started having more fights and problems than we ever had before. Also, I was having more and more episodes of rage attacks. Nothing had changed, except our incidents and my episodes were getting more violent and aggressive. I had become vicious and spewed venom when I raged. When I raged I would loose complete control. Once I started raging, I could not stop and the more I raged the angrier I got. The frenzy I would work myself into would end up in a rage blackout. I had a pattern I had established by this time. I would get angry, lose my temper, boil with anger, yell, scream, rage, loose complete control of my emotions and then go into a raging blackout. I would sometimes hurt myself, but luckily never hurt anyone else.

20.2% of 8th graders, 30.7% of 10th graders, and 42.5% of 12th graders surveyed in 2006 reported that powder cocaine was "fairly easy" or "very easy" to obtain.[59]

I was extremely lucky that I did not hurt anyone else. Often, Bobby was the focus of my crazed attacks, and it was not a positive experience when we had both been drinking and I went off. For example, one night at a party, we got into an argument and I ran out to my car. I knew I was angry and I feared that an uncontrollable raging blackout might ensue. I did not want anyone to see me like that. When I started to drive away, Bobby jumped on the hood of my car and would not get off. I was past the anger stage; I was irate so I stepped on the gas and Bobby flew off of my car. Luckily, he went unhurt except for a cut on his hand. We both were very fortunate that it was not more serious.

Almost 700,000 students between the ages of 18 and 24 are assaulted by another student who has been drinking.[60]

I knew that with the way things were going with Bobby that the relationship had to end, but I did not want to end it. I really did love him, but I was too emotionally sick for it to last. We drifted further apart and I knew it was over but I did not know how to move on. The sky finally came falling down when Bobby got busted and I had my way out of the relationship.

Chapter 14
Lost in My Own Little World

Several of my fraternity brothers and Bobby were in a fraudulent check scam – one that involved the federal government. Somehow they were getting checks from the government sent to them. They would cash the check and keep a percentage of the check. They gave the rest to Rick who organized the process. Rick was one of Bobby's closest friends and also one of the local drug dealers. Rick would keep some of the money and send the rest to whoever was illegally issuing the checks.

When they asked me if I wanted to get a check in my name, I knew that ripping off the federal government was not a good idea. They were not only cashing an illegal check in their own name, but they were also giving their finger print and a photo for identification purposes. That is like a bank robber stopping and giving the teller his social security card and driver's license. Even in my irrational state of mind I knew this was going to end up very badly. I wanted no part of it, and I did not like the idea that so many of my friends were involved.

It did not surprise me when the FBI showed up at the fraternity house. I knew it was about the check con, and I knew that many of my friends were going to be busted and I also knew that with my relationship with Bobby was over. Those who were involved in the rip-off were arrested and charged. It was in the newspapers and on the news. I feared that my parents would find out so I called before they heard it from somewhere else. Trying to explain to your parents how many of your friends and the man you were engaged to were just busted by the FBI was an interesting conversation. I think they were just grateful I had been intuitive enough to stay away from the scam. It was not the fact I was honest; it was the fact I knew they would get caught. If I had been guaranteed there would not have been any negative consequences then I would have been right in the middle of the scam.

On an average day, an estimated 5.3 million convicted offenders were under the supervision of criminal justice authorities. Nearly 40% of these offenders, about 2 million, had been using alcohol at the time of the offense for which they were convicted.[61]

After Bobby was arrested, I was lost in my own little world. I knew we were never going to end up together and I needed to move on. So I moved on very quickly. I did not take any time to mourn the relationship with the man that I was going to marry. It was too painful. If I felt any more darkness inside my soul, I knew I would spontaneously combust. I had seen pictures of people who for no reason just spontaneously combusted into flames. I pondered why it happened. I figured their bodies just could not take in any more sadness and depression so they burst into flames. At the time, my theory seemed plausible and I was waiting for it to happen to me.

Without delay, I jumped into another relationship with a college student named Brent. Since I had no self-esteem and loathed myself, I had to get my validation from outside of myself. Having a boyfriend made me feel accepted and loved. It was the only place I found kudos because I never accepted or loved myself. I know today that only after loving myself and accepting my past and present actions could healthy relationships exist.

The only way I knew how to have a relationship was to meet someone I liked, take them prisoner, and never let them go. For example, I met Brent and he moved into my apartment within a week. Brent was a college football player before he got injured (this impressed me) and he was tall, dark and handsome. We grew up minutes from each other in Richardson and we knew many of the same people. I rationalized that we moved our relationship along quickly because we already knew all about each other. In reality, we knew nothing.

We were both extreme partiers and we drank and drugged together. That was our common bond and that is what brought us together. Brent worked as a doorman at the nightclub near campus, so drugs were always available. I was still very much into the X scene and craved the "Love Drug." Brent did, too. We spent most of our time high on X and/or drinking. The effect of the drug made Brent and I feel like we were madly in love with each other. We could not keep our hands off of each other and we "knew" that we were "destined to be together." X is a very powerful sexual enhancer and mind-altering drug so in less than two months, Brent and I decided we needed to get married and we did. I never considered I was high on X and drunk most of the time I was with him. All we cared about was we were "made for each other."

In 2005, the National Survey on Drug Use and Health reported 502,000 ecstasy users.[62]

My parents were furious I had gotten married and threatened to cut off their financial support. However, their threats did not last long and I soon started graduate school. I was going to get my Masters in Business Administration (MBA.) It was a goal of mine and I was determined to succeed with good grades. Earlier in the year, my father had told me that he did not think I was smart enough to get an MBA and did not want me wasting his money. That was enough motivation for me. I was going to prove him wrong with every fiber of my being.

For the next year and a half, all I did was study, get drunk and get high. My new husband also loved to smoke dope, not my drug of choice. He had a bong that he called the "Enterprise" and whenever anyone smoked out of it we would all yell "Beam me up, Scottie." I could not relate to Brent smoking as much pot as he did because it mellows a person. I preferred sticking with the X or coke that both uplifted my spirits temporarily and gave me an instant jolt of energy.

Adults 18 to 25 years old have the highest rate of current cocaine use, compared to other age groups.[63]

I studied everyday for about 10 hours to get through graduate school. I would sit at our kitchen table with text books and papers strewn everywhere. My mug of Sangria would sit next to me and my pile of coke or crank was not far away. I would go to class at night and then repeat the same cycle over again the next day. Going out during the week became a rare event, but I still had the weekends as my reprieve to party.

If I had a test the next day, I would stay up studying the majority of the night snorting coke. I would sober up during the day to take my test. The first time I did this I wondered if I should snort a line and have a drink before going to class. I was afraid I would not remember anything if I was not high. I figured if I learned and studied the material when I was high maybe I needed to be high to remember it. But I chose not to take this theory to heart and took my tests sober.

Approximately 41% of violent crimes committed against college students and 38% of nonstudents were committed by an offender perceived to be using drugs.[64]

That is how Brent and I made it through our first year of marital paradise. We were wasted the majority of the time. As with all of my relationships, I started having my rage attacks, losing control, yelling, screaming, throwing things and blacking out memories. I understood having blackouts when I was drinking; however, I did not comprehend what was going on with me when I would rage and go into a blackout. This worried me.

Brent was not as empathetic as Bobby was with my rage attacks. One evening we got into a huge fight that ended up in a brawl. As I was losing control of my temper, Brent swung to slap me hit my ear just the right way and I flew to the ground. Something had popped in my head and I could not stand up. I later found out that he had popped my ear drum and I was missing 90% of it. My doctor did not know if I was going to need surgery, so we waited to see if it regenerated on its own. Although my physical body was a mess miraculously my ear drum regenerated. I did not need surgery. There were so many times that God was watching over me and I just did not know it.

Chapter 15
Cocaine Deterioration

I was ecstatic when I graduated and could tell my father that I received my MBA with high grades. If either of us had opened our eyes, we would have seen we were exactly alike. We were highly functioning, raging alcoholics.

My dream was to stay in San Marcos, teach college and continue with my education. The Head of the Business Department was a very caring and wonderful man. He gave me the opportunity to make a presentation to the business department faculty for the position. A few weeks later, they offered me the chance to teach marketing at the university. It was exactly what I wanted to do with my life and I was elated.

My parents were not as joyous as I was about my new opportunity. They did not care that I wanted to teach. They told me that they did not pay for a college and a graduate degree for me to be a teacher. My father insisted that I move home until Brent was finished with school and could move to Dallas. This was one of those times when a person knows that they have come to a fork in the road. I knew what I wanted to do and what was right for me, but financial pressure and fear forced me down the wrong road.

Financially I was not free from my parents because I was not making enough money to survive. Additionally, the teaching position would not start for months. When I talked to my parents, my self-confidence was nil I felt like a little girl cowering again in my toy chest. As a result, I gave up my dream teaching job moved back to Dallas and lived with them temporarily. There was no longer one raging alcoholic in the house now, but two.

I got a job working for a mortgage company and my new career choice seemed to appease my parents. My new job was not what I wanted to be doing, but I was working hard and I was successful. I made an effort never to be home. When I was, I hid in my room and read. Fearing my father and I would have a raging fit at the same time, I avoided him completely. I knew that if we had one of our "episodes" at the same time it would be a serious disaster.

Among the 14 million adults aged 21 or older who were classified as having past year alcohol dependence or abuse, more than 13 million (95%) had started using alcohol before 21 years.[65]

There were a group of co-workers who started meeting for "Happy Hour" a couple times a week so I would meet them. Sometimes we would stay for hours and drink. I seemed to be fitting in fine with corporate America. My drug habit had not stopped and I was using as much cocaine as I always had, but very few people knew.

In a meeting at work, a friend of mine looked at me and handed me a Kleenex. He pointed to my nose and I realized that he was telling me that my nose was bleeding. I excused myself, went to the restroom and knew exactly what was happening. My nose was bleeding because of all the cocaine I had been snorting. Some of my friends had told me they had burned the inside of their noses by snorting so much. Now it was happening to me. My nose was hurting, it was bleeding and I could not get it to stop.

One in ten workers knows someone who uses cocaine on the job.[66]

My bosses and most of the office personnel were not aware of my coke problem so they just thought I had a nose bleed. However, my friend who told me the blood was trickling out of nose took me aside the next day and tried talking to me about it. He knew my nose bleed was caused from my coke addiction, and he was concerned about me. When he looked me in the eyes and told me I needed to get help to stop the drugs, I knew he was being sincere and he was right. He was the first person I remember ever telling me to stop partying the way I did. I knew I needed to stop, but it was completely different when he confronted me about getting help. There was a light that lit in my head and I realized maybe there were options available to help me stop. However, the light was only a flash, and I continued with what I was accustomed.

Brent finished college and moved back to Dallas. We leased a townhome. By this time, I was on the downward slope of my alcoholism and drug addiction. I was constantly drinking during the week and every weekend. If Brent did not want to go, I would go out without him. Brent and I did not live together very long before our fighting became an issue. Since we both were using and drinking perpetually and because of my raging and resentments, our relationship was short-lived.

We split up within a few short months. Like the other times that I had broke up with someone, I did not hesitate for a moment to find someone else. Taking time for me was not an option. I did not like myself and I feared what I would find if I had to look within. There was a man named Jacob who I knew from high school and who had been going out regularly with the group I hung out with. He always seemed to have a supply of coke or X so I naturally drifted to spending more time with him.

Chapter 16
Deadly Drunk Depression

Even though I was dating Jacob, the break-up of my marriage had more of a toll on me than I would admit to myself or anyone else. I felt like a complete loser and it confirmed I could not do anything right. I was depressed and hated myself more than ever. One evening, a group of friends were going clubbing and I was getting dressed up. I tried to look perfect from the outside, because I felt so dead on the inside. When I was dressing, I looked in the mirror at myself and could not stand the reflection. I looked at myself snorting a rail of coke. Staring back at me was someone who I did not know at all. My own reflection was too much for me to handle. I quickly picked up my coke, tucked it in my purse and ran out the door. I did not want to see the reflection of the person I had become.

A Little Sister friend of mine from college had also moved to Dallas when she graduated and she joined our party group. Tori and I had been drinking buddies for several years, and it was great having her in Dallas. We immediately took up where we left off and there was never a lack of drugs. We would rent limos and go out for the evening. I could lie and tell you that we had gotten smart and did not what to be driving drunk, but the truth was we liked the celebrity attention we received when we pulled up to a club in a limo. By the end of the night, we would have a limo full of friends with drugs ready to stay awake all night long.

Everything was catching up to me and I noticed alcohol did not have the numbing effect it had on me for so many years. I could drink and drink, but I could not get the same buzz. The effect had changed and I did not like that at all. Cocaine also seemed to be lacking its "sparkle" it once had. I was beyond the point of no return.

I was home alone in my townhome and I was drinking a bottle of champagne by myself. Suddenly, I was awakened by my dog barking and jumping on me. There was smoke everywhere, and I did not know what was happening. Then I remembered I had lit the fireplace before I started drinking and figured I had passed out. I could barely see through the smoke, but I crawled to the door and then opened all the windows. The fireplace was still billowing smoke as I realized I had not opened the flue. The smoke had no where to go except into the house. The smoke was clearing slightly as I managed to slowly creep over to the fireplace. I opened it. It was hot and I burned my hand, but I was grateful the fire had not spread outside the fireplace.

Between 48% and 64% of people who die in fires have blood alcohol levels indicating intoxication.[67]

After the smoke cleared, the soot from the smoke was all over the walls, the bricks, the carpet and the furniture. My dog, Tosha, had saved me from my alcohol induced sleep. I was grateful my dog was safe, but I really did not care that I had not died from smoke inhalation. Depression was completely taking over my body both physically and mentally. I speculated if I would be better off dead instead of having to suffer with the empty and useless feelings consuming me.

About the same time, Tori had experienced fall out from her disease as well. Not only did she drink and drug the same way I did, but she had an eating disorder. She had anorexia and bulimia. Our partying had contributed to her eating disorder resurfacing. Tori was an itty-bitty little thing and had been in treatment before for her problem; however, she was now displaying serious signs of having it again in full force. Tori's blackouts were not from drinking or raging like mine; her blackouts occurred with food. Once she started binging and purging, it eventually would graduate to her having eating blackouts. Tori would go to bed and wake up the next morning to find herself asleep in her kitchen with food all over the place. The oven and stove would be on with food burning and overflowing. She would have no recollection of what had happened.

About 1% of female adolescents have anorexia. That means that about one out of every one hundred young women between ten and twenty are starving themselves.[68]

I went over to her apartment one morning to wake her. I found her lying in the kitchen in the middle of a sea of food. It was half eaten and thrown all over the apartment. She had no idea what had happened during the night.

Tori knew she was in trouble. If she kept going in the direction she was headed with the alcohol, drugs and food she would die. She told her parents and they immediately sent her to rehabilitation (rehab) for her addictions. There she would get the help she needed to survive. This was the first close friend who went to rehab and it was the first time it registered in my brain there was help available for my problems. This was a pivotal moment in my alcoholism because I began thinking about getting help for myself.

About 4% or four out of one hundred, college-aged women have bulimia. About 50% of people who have been anorexic develop bulimia or bulimic patterns.[69]

Jacob and I were still together. However, like all my past relationships, we were fighting terribly. Only a short time after Tori went to rehab, I hit my bottom. I was curled up in the fetal position in my apartment with all the shades closed, all the lights turned off, a candle burning, and listening to Yaz on the stereo. Yaz was a depressing tape sent to me by my high school buddy Ryan, who now had AIDs. I knew this was the end for me. I was hoping that if I just stayed rocking in the fetal position that I would die, but I did not. I knew I could not take another snort of coke, hit of X, or drink of alcohol anymore. I knew if I continued on my path of addictive destruction I would die within the year. The more I used drugs, the more I wanted; the more I drank the more I wanted. It was never enough to satisfy my urges and it was never enough to stop the gut wrenching pain I felt.

Jacob came over to my apartment and found me sobbing uncontrollably on the floor in the dark. We agreed I needed help and I needed it immediately. I called my mother and was honest with her. It was one of the few times in my life I had been completely honest with my mother. I told her I needed to go to rehab because I was a cocaine addict. My mother and Jacob helped organize my insurance in order, find an inpatient rehab in the area, and get me admitted. I had short term disability at work so I was paid while I was not working. I had no idea what to expect, but all I knew was I needed something in my life to change. I could not live with this kind of depression any longer.

Chapter 17
Breaking the Cycle

There were two sections of the hospital, one was the psych ward and the other side was the alcohol and drug treatment. I was put on the psych ward. This made me angry because I said I was not crazy. I needed help for my cocaine addiction. The admitting doctor said I needed both treatments, and that I would be going to the group meetings in both wards. The last thing I was going to do was admit I belonged on the psych ward, but deep down I knew that my depression, raging and thoughts of suicide qualified me.

In 2003, a total of 28,723 persons died from drug-induced causes in the United States. Drug-induced causes in the United States includes not only deaths from legal and illegal drug use, but also poisoning from medically prescribed and other drugs.[70]

Once admitted to my room in rehab all I did was lay in bed. My body must have known I was in a safe place, and it just gave out. I lay in bed contemplating how my life had gone so askew. I sleep most of the first week, except when they would come get me for group meetings.

The first time someone told me that I was an alcoholic and a drug addict who was going to be put into a 12 step program, I thought they were the certifiable ones. I knew I had a drug problem and I grasped the concept I was an addict. I knew I would have to abstain from drugs, but I did not comprehend the fact I was an alcoholic also. The idea of giving up drinking alcohol for the rest of my life was unfathomable. Giving up alcohol was not an option in my mind. That's when I had a moment of clarity and saw the irony of what I was thinking. If I could not picture my life without alcohol, I had to concede I was an alcoholic. I also knew alcohol was a drug and if I had a problem with drugs, alcohol was included in that equation.

The doctors explained to me alcoholism was a progressive and hereditary disease of mental and physical obsession. All of this information was new to me and I was baffled. When I heard alcoholism was hereditary, that explained so much of my family dysfunction. Alcoholism is a family disease and goes from one generation to the next. If the family never seeks any kind of help the family's dysfunctional behaviors will be passed along also. My family had alcoholism as far back as I could remember and no one ever stepped out of the familiar chaos to find a different way of living. It is so much easier to continue in our miserable everyday lives than to break the cycle and get help. Once you are in the dysfunction, you begin to believe that everybody's families include raging, drunken stupors and belittling commentaries. It is easier to accept how you are living this way.

Once I had acquired this information on alcoholism and drug addiction I knew I could fix myself. At least I thought so when I told everyone that I did not have to stay in the hospital. I now understood what was wrong with me, and I believed I could stop drinking and using on my own. The other alcoholics and addicts in rehab thought this was the most hilarious thing they had ever heard and laughed hysterically at me. They assured me if I had been capable of stopping my addictions on my own I would have done so the first time I drank and got sick. Their attitudes were rude and I did not like being laughed at, but I knew deep down they were right and I stayed.

The rehab took all the drunks and druggies to Alcoholics Anonymous (AA) and Narcotics Anonymous (NA) meetings. I had heard of AA on television; however, I knew nothing about it and really did not give a crap because I was clinically depressed. The first support group meeting was a speaker meeting. I was told to listen for similarities. When I saw the speaker was an old man who claimed to have many years of sobriety, I rolled my eyes and declared out loud that I could not possibly have anything in common with this old guy. It turned out that I was dead wrong.

Estimated Alcoholics Anonymous groups throughout the world in 2006: 106,202.[71] (There is no practical way of counting meetings, this estimate is considered to be extremely low.)

As he started telling his story I heard how he once had the same intense feelings of sadness I had, and he thought the same way that I did. He also had the same kind of drunken stupors I had experienced, and he was also a drug addict. My attitude began to soften and I listened intently. The other people at the meeting were laughing at the man's story and having fun. I could not believe all of these people were alcohol and drug free, but they were. I tried to remember the last time I had laughed and truly had fun like these sober alcoholics and I could not recall a time.

I had never heard anyone sum up my personal life experiences while telling their own as the old man speaking had. I was comforted internally to know other people could not stop drinking and also loved drugs as much as I had. Another moment of clarity and relief consumed me. There was not a doubt in my mind; I was in the right place with the right people.

Estimated Narcotics Anonymous groups throughout the world in 2007: over 25,065 groups holding over 43,900 meetings in 127 countries.[72] (There is no practical way of counting meetings, this estimate is considered to be extremely low.)

Since I had not been using coke and had not consumed any alcohol for about a week, my body and mind was craving it. Alcohol and drugs had been apart of my daily life for so long and I still longed for it. My body was continuing to detox even though my shaking and puking had stopped.

Chronic heavy alcohol consumption exacts a greater physical toll on women than on men. Female alcoholics have death rates 50% to 100% higher than those of male alcoholics. A greater percent of female alcoholics also die from suicides, alcohol-related injuries, circulatory disorders, and cirrhosis of the liver.[73]

The more support group meetings I attended, the more I wondered how the people there could be so full of energy and life. Since I was 15, I had used alcohol and drugs to have fun and to create what I thought was a good time. I had no idea what I was going to do now.

I was definitely not having fun. The emptiness and void inside my soul was too much to bear. All I felt was immense sadness surrounded by a huge black hole inside me. The alcohol and drugs were not there to fill it anymore or to help push my feeling back down inside. As a result, my feelings were pouring out of me. I was overwhelmed with sorrow, regret, and uselessness. I was drowning in the flood of emotions overpowering me.

The worst part was I felt hopeless. I was scared I was going to have to live feeling dejected and depressed forever. I could not see how I would ever even get out of bed and function in society. I kept thinking that it had to get better tomorrow. However, everyday I woke up and felt like I was in more emotional pain than the day before. It was debilitating. I did not know where all the pain was coming from and did not understand how I could have possibly been holding all this in for so long. It was gushing out and I knew even drugs and alcohol at this point could not have stopped it. All I could do was lie in bed in hideous agony.

30% of women are depressed. Men's figures were previously thought to be half that of women, but new estimates are higher.[74]

Chapter 18
Spontaneous Combustion

This went on for a few 3 weeks and I could not take it anymore. So, I got up and walked out the front door without telling anyone. I walked and walked and just kept walking for hours. I was furious at myself and the situation I was in and the exercise seemed to help a little. I walked to my apartment, got the leasing office to open my door, and then hung out for awhile. I knew people would be worrying about me, so I called my mother and Jacob to let them know where I was. They immediately took me back to the hospital even though I threw a fit of resistance. Once again, my spontaneous combustion theory came to mind. I thought I would burst into flames or my head would explode if I had to stay in treatment any longer.

I was adamant about leaving. Thus, I made an agreement with my mother to go to intensive outpatient treatment and support group meetings everyday for 90 days. I left rehab and began my next phase of treatment.

Even with the absence of my mind, I knew there was only one hope to get out of this miserable depression. I would need therapy and support group meetings. That is exactly what I did because I knew I would rather die than live the way I felt for the rest of my life. I found a support group close to my apartment and went to 3 meetings a day for 90 days. Therapy sessions were 3 to 4 times a week with my psychologist.

Depressive disorders affect approximately 18.8 million American adults or about 9.5% of the U.S. population age 18 and older in a given year.[75]

Some days it was too much for me to pull myself out of bed. Friends from my support group would come over, get me up, throw me in the shower and bring me to the meeting. I went to three meetings a day because I would have done anything to stay away from alcohol and drugs. I knew the people at the meetings were already sober and happy. I figured I might as well try listening to them. It was the only shot I had at changing my life and hopefully helping my depression. Going back to drinking and drugging were not the answer and I knew it.

My head was in a fog for the first 6 months. I had no idea what I was doing and I just kept going back to my support group. My friends told me to make coffee, take out the trash, clean the ash trays, and pick up the coffee cups. That is exactly what I did. Anything to keep me occupied and out of the bars. I did not know what to do with myself because drinking and drugging took up so much of my time and entertainment. Without it, I was lost. Alcohol and drugs were my two best friends. Now they were gone, along with all my using buddies. Once your "using" friends know you were put in rehab they also know you do not have any more drugs. Most disappear very quickly.

Physically, I felt atrocious and my mind was like mush. I kept forgetting how to do basic tasks. I felt like I had a maturity level of a 10 year-old little girl. I believe that alcoholics and addicts stop maturing when we starting drinking and using, so feeling like a 10 year-old girl was appropriate. Depression and anxiety ruled my first several months of sobriety. I kept going to therapy and my support group. However, all I wanted to do was die. Dying had to be easier than having cravings or obsessing constantly, but I hung on.

15% of depressed people will commit suicide.[76]

My support group seemed very strange to me at first. But I did what they suggested. I had no problem realizing and admitting I was an alcoholic and an addict I was utterly insane. No one keeps doing the same things I did repeatedly without being completely crazed. The problem was I did not believe I could recover from the emotional state I was in.

Jacob and I were still dating during my first several months of recovery. I was holding on to our relationship for dear life. I had let go of most of old friends, quit going to clubs, and stopped drinking and using. There was no way I was going to give up Jacob too. Not only did I not think I could not live by myself, but I literally thought that I would die if Jacob left. He was the only thing I had semi-filling that big black hole I had in my gut. So I insanely held on to him with all my might. Jacob continued drinking and using and had the same lifestyle we had before I went to rehab. My codependency regarding him was growing more and more extreme everyday along with my insanity. He refused to get sober and I refused to let go.

Finally, Jacob left because he knew it was not ever going to work with me sober and him still drinking and drugging. I give him credit for helping to save my life. Jacob never hesitated to get me help and encourage me to go to rehab. He also knew he had to leave me or I would never recover fully.

Chapter 19
Reality in "Sobriety Land"

Even without alcohol and drugs my thinking and behaviors were irrational. I was still having raging fits. Panic attacks became a regular part of my week. If I went places, I would often have panic attacks where I felt like I could not move and could not catch my breath. I would shake and cry until I could be calmed down. The only place I felt comfortable outside of my apartment was with my support group.

80% of depressed people are not currently receiving any treatment.[77]

I was ready to kill myself after Jacob left because I could not stand the emotional pain. All of my abandonment issues and childhood abuse I had never dealt with were surfacing. It was too strenuous for me to stay by myself in my apartment. When I was alone, I had no distractions and I had to face myself. I had no idea I would feel as horrendous as I did being sober for several months. I was grateful I could not comprehend the extent of emotional misery a person goes through to get sober. If I had known this in rehab I may have made other choices. However, I was into this thing called sobriety and dealing with my past required me remaining clean and sober. I had to do it or I knew I would die.

There was a divine lady named Sammy who was the secretary at the support group. She answered phones all day at the club. I sat with her day after day because I liked her and that is all I was capable of doing at the time. Sammy had a warm, caring smile and she would say, "AJ, you just keep coming back because we are going to *love you back to life*!" Then she would laugh and say, "And you need a whole lotta loving." She then would throw her arms around me and give me a big hug that warmed my heart. I loved Sammy and I knew she loved me. She meant what she said. I had never truly felt unconditional love until I met my support group friends and they were never lacking in it. They loved and cared about me and did not want anything in return. They wanted what was best for me and would do anything to help me stay sober and clean.

I wish I could say after a year of being alcohol and drug free all was perfect in "Sobriety Land," but what happened to me would be far from the truth. Living life on life's terms was not agreeing with me. I wanted to be different and I wanted to change everything I did not like about myself instantly, but I could not. It was a struggle emotionally to cope. Physically my body was still healing and I was astonished when I grew almost two inches the first year after rehab. The doctor told me since I started using so young I may have stunted my growth and now I was getting healthier physically as it was catching up.

It is suggested as part of many support groups that an alcoholic and/or addict participate in the 12 Steps of Recovery. As part of working the steps, I was told to make a list of everyone I had resentments against and everyone I had harmed in my using years. I thought they had to be jesting. I believed I had resentments against everyone I had ever met since the first grade, especially the nun who made me pee in my panties. If I had to be honest, I would also have to include God on my resentment list because for so long I despised him. There was absolutely no way I could make a list that long and even remember every person. I could not tell another person I despised God and was angry at him for giving me a raging alcoholic father, a codependent mother and the cursing disease of alcoholism. I blamed God for all my childhood abuse and severely dysfunctional home.

But deep down inside I wanted to do the task. If doing the assignment could relieve some of my pain then I was desperate to do it. I made a list of all my resentments and everyone I had hurt. I wrote and wrote for weeks on end. Everyone I could possibly think of who I bore a grudge was written down. I did not want to leave anyone off or forget anything because I was told my sobriety hinged on my honesty. My sponsor kept insisting we are only as sick as our secrets.

***Depression results in more absenteeism than almost any other physical disorder and costs employers more than $51 billion per year in absenteeism and lost productivity.*[78]**

I did the best resentment list I could possibly do at the time and explained my part in each scenario. It was important for me to understand I needed to look at only what my part was, not what others had (or what I thought they had done to me.) It took me weeks to complete and emotionally it was extremely draining. I was exhausted. I felt like I had just purged my guts all over the paper. But I did it and I was relieved not only because I was finished, but also because I felt a sense of relief.

My therapist was the first to hear me read my resentments out loud. It took several sessions, but we felt it was important for him to hear everything about me if he was going to be guiding me. I also read it to my first support group sponsor and I truly felt a sense of relief and freedom for the first time in my life. Now, other people knew the horrendous things I had done when I was drinking and using and they still accepted me. They also told me I was going to be alright. They reminded me that other alcoholics and addicts had made the same bad decisions and I was not alone in the sobriety journey. They also explained I needed to start forgiving myself for my past indiscretions.

Chapter 20
Perception of Power

A major part of getting sober for me was to discover a Higher Power, whoever or whatever that may be, to rely on. My Higher Power all my life was God, but my problem was I believed God hated and doomed me to hell by the third grade. Being raised in a strict Catholic Church, it took me many years to realize the church had taught us forgiveness, but those parts of the teachings never registered in my brain. My perception was God had already written me off as a bad apple so I was hopeless.

Chronic or life-long depression is caused by trauma in childhood which includes: emotional, physical or sexual abuse; yelling or threats or abuse; neglect; criticism; family addiction; and violence in the family to mention just a few.[79]

My support group friends taught me a new Higher Power and a God of my own understanding. I listened to how they trusted and loved their God and I wanted to have that kind of relationship with mine. The more I listened, the more my insight into God changed. My Higher Power became loving, caring, kind, and, best of all, forgiving. I grew to trust my new God and to believe he wanted what was best for me. Once my feelings toward God started to transform then I personally began slowly changing my actions and attitudes.

Gradually I started doing activities that normies (normal or non-addicts) do. I went to the movies, art festivals, window shopping at the mall, and parties (without alcohol or drugs) at my new friends' homes. Everyone was very patient with me because sometimes we would go somewhere and I would have a massive panic attack. My heart would start racing and I could not breathe. Then I would have to go home. However, slowly my panic episodes diminished and they finally went away after about a year and a half of sobriety.

At first, it felt odd not going clubbing on the weekends and I was embarrassed to be seen at the movies on a Friday or Saturday night. In my mind it was just not the "cool" place to be. I learned what other people thought of me was not of any consequence. This was part of my lack of self-esteem and I had to let go of other people's opinions of me. All that mattered was what I thought about myself.

My recovery was a very slow process. I was the poster child for the old adage "Never Say Never" because everything that did not happen to me while I was drinking and drugging occurred in the first several years of my sobriety. I was laid off my job, arrested, utilities were shut off, my car was repossessed, and I filed bankruptcy. I was not exactly a recovery Honor Student.

Even though I was not using drugs or drinking, there came a time when I had to make some severe changes in the quality of my personal recovery. I threw myself more into meetings, talking to my sponsor and doing community service. Even though I had not been drinking or drugging, I believe I hit a bottom in sobriety. Therefore, I had to change or eventually my disease would win.

For many years in my sobriety, men and sex served as devices I used to fill the void still haunting me inside. All I wanted to do was temporarily fill the emptiness that often still throbbed with pain. However, I did notice the hollowness within me was not as intensely painful as it had once been. It was a process, but my internal empty space was being filled with my new faith in my higher power, new friends and my support group.

Getting out of bed became easier for me and I did not lie in bed as often. I was functioning in the real world better than I ever had. Even though I had made many, many mistakes and there was a lot of room for improvement, I knew I was feeling better physically and emotionally. My progress may have been at a turtle's pace, but I could finally see changes in my life and that kept me in recovery. It was easier for me to notice changes in other people than in myself. This gave me hope it would happen for me, and it eventually did.

The obsession to drink and use drugs was not as consuming or unrelenting anymore and the craving had diminished along with many of my fears. I was beginning to have some semblance of self-confidence and began thinking about other people for a change. Everyone and everything did not revolve around me anymore.

Alcoholics Anonymous members were three times more likely to be abstinent a year after their first treatment for alcoholism, compared to individuals who received no support.[80]

Chapter 21
Codependency Run Amuck

"When a couple becomes enmeshed, that is, when the individualities of each partner are sacrificed to the relationship, the individuals and the partnership suffer. Sometimes, one partner forces the other to give up separate opinions, perspectives, and preferences. If a childhood is used for survival, then little energy is left to develop a separate sense of self. It's likely, then, that a person who had to spend childhood surviving would enter marriage as an incomplete person. She'd be vulnerable to absorbing her mate's perspectives, ideas, and attitudes and taking them as her own."[81]
Taken from the book, Boundaries, Where You End and I Begin. By: Anne Katherine, MA

I was jolted into a reality check that alcoholism is a deadly disease and many people do not make it in recovery. A gorgeous teenage girl, Mia, who had lived with me temporarily and I loved dearly, committed suicide. She was an alcoholic/addict and had struggled for many years trying to stay sober, but I never imagined that she would kill herself. Her tragedy was a result of a combination of addiction and codependency run amuck. When her boyfriend moved away and they broke up, she could not stand the pain of losing him. Tragically, she placed a plastic bag over her head, and suffocated herself. I can empathize with the agony she felt when loosing someone and the torment she was feeling. Mia had the same feelings I felt when Jacob left me, and I thought I was going to die. I believed with every fiber of my being I could not live without him. Mia must have felt the same way.

Codependency is just as dangerous and deadly as alcoholism and drug addiction if left untreated. The combination can be like a time bomb ticking and waiting to detonate. One way to explain codependency is a state when all your personal boundaries are disregarded and you lose yourself to someone else. Your life completely revolves around the other person. If they are happy, then you are. If they are sad, then you are. A codependent's feelings are based on how another person is feeling or acting. You lose total sight of your own personal feelings and take on someone else's. As a result, if they leave then you feel like you are losing yourself. In a way you are because for a long time you allowed their thoughts and actions to define your self. When they are gone, you lose all perspective and are faced with the feelings that your self no longer exists. It is excruciatingly painful when the person you depend on for your self worth leaves because a codependent feels even more worthless than ever.

In the United States there is a suicide every 17 minutes or 83 suicides a day.[82]

Hundreds of people showed up for Mia's death. A teenage alcoholic, addict, and codependent, who thought no one loved her, had touched so many lives and was loved by so many. It forced me to realize when I am in the lowest depression and think I am alone and unloved; it is not the true reality of the situation. I may feel that way at that moment, but the truth is I am loved by many and my life affects many others positively.

Kalvin was also a friend I became close to in rehab and he was having problems staying clean and sober. After rehab we hung out often and went to meetings together a lot. As I struggled to stay sober the first couple of years of sobriety, Kalvin kept having brief set backs by using and drinking periodically. When he would start acquiring a few months of sobriety, he would drift back to his old habits. When I called him, I was never sure if he was going to be drunk or sober. Kalvin came from an upper-income family and not only had financial support, but also emotional support from his parents and siblings to stay sober. But this does not guarantee sobriety and Kalvin kept playing with the deadly disease.

40% of those who started drinking at age 13 or younger developed alcohol dependence later in life. 10% of teens who began drinking after the age of 17 developed dependence.[83]

I often said I never had to start drinking or using again, because Kalvin was doing it for me. I observed his guilt and remorse time after time when he would walk back into the support group after a slip.

One evening I received a call from Kalvin and my answering machine picked up. He was drunk and could barely speak and mumbled some gibberish into the machine. I did not answer the phone and did not call him back that evening. I waited a couple of days and called him. After trying to reach him for a couple of weeks, I gave up calling. I figured he was out on one of his binges and would call me when he wanted to sober up. Kalvin never called again. Several months had passed and I just assumed Kalvin was still partying, but I learned Kalvin had overdosed and died. That explained why I had not heard from him. Even though I knew Kalvin was playing with death with every drink and drug he took, I never wanted to think about the consequences. I assumed he would eventually get clean and sober. I was not expecting his life to end up being such a misfortune. He had so much to offer and he wasted and destroyed his own life. Alcoholism is such a shrewd and inexplicably deadly disease.

It is often said suicide is the most selfish thing you can do. When a person is in a depressed alcohol-induced state they forget how many people love them and care about them. They believe they are completely hopeless and there is nothing that will help. All they can feel is excruciating emotional pain. Kalvin executed the ultimate selfish task and killed himself. His family and friends were shattered and Kalvin was gone forever.

In the United States, there are over 30,000 deaths from suicide annually with 12 of every 100,000 American killing themselves.[84]

Over the years, I have wondered if Kalvin died the night he had called me when I had let the answering machine pick up. I have no way of knowing. The fact I will never know if I could have been of service to a fellow alcoholic and friend is something I have to live with. Even though I realize I could not have "fixed" Kalvin and his problems, experience taught me a very valuable lesson - to always do my best to help other alcoholics when they are in need.

For many other friends in recovery, their journeys also ended in death, for example: more overdoses, drunk driving accidents, complications of prolonged abuse, and death from the disease of alcoholism itself. I quickly learned the sadly alarming fact about alcoholism and recovery…not everyone makes it. This was another recurring reminder that alcoholism is a deadly disease and I now feared playing with death. I had so little regard for life for so long and I was awakening to the concept life was worth living.

The odds of committing suicide are almost two times greater if you drink than if you don't, even if you do not drink to excess.[85]

Chapter 22
Living Amends

It was time to expand my horizons and start going to other support groups instead of constantly going to the same one. I started going to other groups because it was important I heard different alcoholics and addicts share their recovery and sobriety. Once you are in a support group, you learn they are everywhere and have meetings often. I went to halfway houses, women's hospitals, inner city groups, and the experience allowed me to realize there is a whole world of people who are involved in recovery. Although it was important to keep my home group, venturing out of my comfort zone and meeting a vast array of different sober people allowed me to grow as an individual and prosper spiritually.

The prevalence of alcoholism is more than twice as high (19%) among those who have suffered from depression at some time during their lives as those who have not (9%).[86]

The other women in the support groups became a safe haven for me. I usually had male friends before sobriety and getting close to women was difficult at first. Deep down I believed the women would never understand my drinking and drug habits and I feared they would judge me. But I finally let the walls I had built around me be discarded brick by brick. The women became my friends and safety net. I recognized I was not different from them and breaking through my fears revealed the complete opposite of what I was expecting. I found I related to groups of women and found more likenesses than I could ever have imagined. We had all experienced and struggled as women alcoholics and all had the same goal…to stay sober.

After years of sobriety, the obsession to drink and drug was gone. It was no longer an option in my life. I pray I never forget the hideously dreadful feelings engulfing me in rehab and my first years of sobriety. I do not ever want to forget the black pit of emptiness in my soul now filled with love and my faith and trust in my Higher Power. I truly believe remembering those feelings, even though I had to let go of them, has helped me remain clean and sober.

590,759 females were admitted to treatment facilities in the United States during 2005, representing 31.9% of the total treatment admissions.[87]

My dysfunctional parents were also slowly changing. As my father grew older, he quit smoking and because of health issues slowed down considerably in his beer consumption. I kept my distance for many years from my parents and would visit periodically and on the required holidays. However, my mother had started going to Alanon meetings (a 12 step program for families of alcoholics) and had made some very special friends who also had husbands and children who were alcoholics. Changes in my mother's behaviors were dramatic and we started to become friends. My father had retired and my mother knew that staying home with him everyday would not be in her best interest, so she found a part time job and started working. She met new friends and started going places and having a better social life than she had in years. My mother no longer waited around jumping to my father's every whim; she was enjoying life.

Once I was able to let go of the past and forgive my parents, our relationships changed. It took many years, but with both my mother and I in our recovery programs, we became real friends for the first time in our lives. My father and I found a middle ground and were also enjoying each others company. He never wanted to admit I was an alcoholic, but he had no problem admitting I had a drug problem. This is how he rationalized me being active in a recovery program. He also never admitted he personally had a problem; he knew my mother was going to Alanon, only because I was the alcoholic in the family. Denial is an amazing part of alcoholism and keeps millions of people from ever getting sober and finding true happiness.

In my early 30s and to my family's surprise, my father was diagnosed with esophagus cancer. The doctor said all his years of drinking and smoking had most likely contributed to the cancer. He underwent an investigative type of surgery and they removed his esophagus and stretched his stomach and attached it to his throat. He also underwent chemotherapy and radiation treatments that irritated his throat even more. Eating was impossible for him and he had to be hooked up to a feeding tube every night. My mother had extreme difficulties cleaning the tubes and attaching the tubes throughout the day, so I moved home during the week. For the next year, I was home on week days taking care of my father; on the weekends I would operate a clothing store I had opened in Deep Ellum, Dallas.

There are more deaths, illnesses and disabilities from substance abuse than from any other preventable health condition. [88]

I thanked my Higher Power everyday for my sobriety, but now I was more grateful than ever I was able to be there for my parents. Never in my wildest imagination would I ever have thought I would not only be able to help my parents, but want to help them. The fact I honestly cared and wanted to be there for both of them was a miracle only possible because I was clean and sober. It was the first time I had experienced someone slowly dying. The deaths I had encountered in the past were unexpected but quick; this was completely different. To watch someone who was 250 pounds, lose about half of that weight in 8 months is a strenuous experience. Seeing first hand someone in the physical agonizing pain he was in was not only unbearable for him, but also for my mother and me. Towards the end of his decline, we could not touch him because he would scream insufferable cries. The cancer had progressed to his bones and it was excruciating.

Heavy drinking contributes to illness in each of the top three causes of death: heart disease, cancer and stroke. [89]

A year after his surgery my father passed on. I was the only person with him when he died and I was able to be there for him, give him loving comfort and hold his hand as he died. By forgiving the past and being of service to him, I was able to briefly get to know him in a different light during the year he was ill. When he passed we were at peace with each other. I had always loved him, but it was only because he was my father. Now I truly loved him because I had the opportunity to get to know him. I knew I had made living amends to my father and I was blessed.

Heavy drinking can increase the risk for certain cancers, especially those of the liver, esophagus, throat and larynx (voice box). [90]

Chapter 23
The "Lush" Life

After my father's death, I began concentrating on the work in my clothing store. It was barely scraping by, and without prior notice, the local off beat paper I advertised in weekly refused to take my advertisement. They said the night club style clothes were too wild and sexy; they were cleaning up their paper. Apparently, they were in the process of being bought out and they did not want to offend anyone.

I did not know where I was going to advertise and I was angry. In a huge city like Dallas there were not any positive options. Fortunately, I had been writing a few press releases and articles for some of the local Dallas magazines and business papers. I was explaining to Herald who was the owner of one of the papers about my advertising dilemma. He suggested that we start our own entertainment paper and target all the controversial advertisers that were not allowed to advertise in the mainstream media.

I knew it was a great idea. It would give me a place to advertise the store. I was so angry. My cute sexy advertisement was not permitted in the other paper any longer. I immediately said that I would do it. If I had thought for a split second about what I was getting myself into, I may not have had the guts to go through with it.

Between all my customers and contacts with night club owners, and with Herald's newspaper knowledge, in a few short weeks we printed our first monthly edition. The first year he was not active with the new publication but gave me direction and advice. I worked relentlessly on making it a success. It was perfect timing in the market place because many businesses were looking for places to advertise and thankfully we were one of the few options they had.

The business quickly boomed and I could no longer work with only a couple of employees. Herald saw the money the paper was making and knew he had hit the gold mine with this venture. He sold his other business publication and came to work with me full-time.

The business exploded with advertisers and we were becoming very popular with the night clubs. Our staff was growing and we hired experienced sales people and my boyfriend, Tony, came to work for us. It was like we had won the lottery because the money was pouring in. Advertisers were begging us to print weekly and we listened to what they wanted. We started printing weekly and then expanded to three different weekly publications throughout the state.

During this time, I remained clean and sober. However, I was not going to as many meetings or keeping as close to my support group as I should have. My excuse was the business was keeping me too busy and I did not have the time. The truth was I was overwhelmed with my success and had money for expensive things I never dreamed. I bought a beautiful house on a golf course with a pool and hot tub, and a brand new Porsche. I was happy and having an incredible time and placed my recovery on the back burner.

Chapter 24
Addiction Chaos

Everything seemed to be going along great. The company kept growing and expanding into different avenues. Herald and I were getting along and I felt like I could trust him with my life. But after a few short years of bliss, Herald's drinking became a serious problem. Advertisers were calling me and complaining he had made scenes in their clubs and they were going to pull their advertising. Herald had never been exposed to the kind of lifestyle the gentlemen's clubs offered. He was like a little boy in a candy store and he could not get enough. The drinking led to drugs and he started using cocaine regularly and had regular mistresses. Herald's personality completely changed and the only thing he was concerned about was money and partying. The Herald I had met and worked with for several years was happily married with two children who were the center of his life. That Herald was long gone and I could not believe that I was dealing with another sick alcoholic and addict in my life.

15 million heavy drinkers hold full-time jobs where they pose serious problems for the health, well-being and productivity of everyone around them.[91]

I was long past being frustrated with Herald's behaviors. Even though I was not drinking or drugging my actions and reactions were becoming just as bad as his behaviors because I was not regularly going to my support group. As Herald's addiction was heightening (he was using cocaine regularly) so was my rage. Even though my rage had subsided for long periods of time, since I was not going to my support group like I should have been. Thus, I was not dealing with my negative emotions and they would burst out inappropriately.

Herald and I started to fight constantly and he started undermining everything I was doing. Looking back, I now realize he was setting me up for his future plans. Even though Herald and I were not getting along and the negativity in the office was unbearable, it never occurred to me to continue the company without him.

As we acquired more and more money and grew bigger and bigger Herald's greed grew. I should have been more in tune with what a practicing addict and alcoholic was capable of doing, but I always trusted my partner. Although we were constantly arguing, I never questioned that we both wanted what was best for the company. I was definitely wrong. Like any alcoholic and addict in denial, Herald loathed me getting upset with his drinking and drugging. He wanted to continue doing what he was doing without me hassling him and without us fighting. I continually asked him to get help or check into a hospital, but he refused.

Employees who use drugs miss work more often, are less healthy, and are more prone to harming themselves and others in the workplace.[92]

Another huge problem started because Herald was drinking and drugging with some of the employees and one of them was involved in an accident. I was furious because now Herald's actions were jeopardizing the company with law suits. Unbeknownst to me, Herald was devising a plan to oust me from the company. In his alcoholic mind, he rationalized he could get rid of me and keep all the money.

I should have been more cautious of a practicing alcoholic and realized the way I was nagging him and the way we were arguing would eventually cause him to snap. Practicing alcoholics and addicts have no moral standards and all they care about is their own well-being. I should have remembered this, because I had been like him many years earlier. But somehow, the longer a recovering alcoholic is away from drugs and alcohol you tend to forget what it is completely like.

Herald underhandedly convinced about half of the employees in the office that he was going to get rid of me and either take over the paper or put it out of business. He was a master con artist and he worked on the employees for along time by wining and dining them, drinking and drugging with them and offering raises and bonuses. So when he devised a plan to get rid of me, he had all of the employees who drank and used drugs convinced I needed to go. The other half of the employees were clean and sober and in recovery and he knew he would never have a chance of manipulating them like he had the others.

Drug users also had far higher job turnover rates with 12.3% reporting they had worked for three or more employers in the past year, compared with 5.1% of non-abusing workers.[93]

After an event we held in Houston one weekend, Herald set his plan into motion.When I went to the office on Monday morning, everything was gone. He had taken all the client books, wiped out the computer and phone systems, the layout boards were gone and even the phones were gone. I found out Herald had moved half of the employees up the street and were planning on producing the paper there.The former employees were already calling clients and telling them my company was out of business. I was devastated and dumbfounded. I could see how Herald could have conned some of the employees but I had no idea how or what he had said or promised to some of them. One of the employees who left had worked in my clothing stores for years and I always considered him family.There was another young man who I had "adopted" when he had no where to live and I opened my home to him. Still another was a sorority sister from college who could not find a job and had been working small jobs when I hired her. However, she drank and drugged with Herald so her actions did not surprise me when I pondered the scenario. I knew he could easily manipulate her under these conditions.

One of the most frustrating factors in dealing with alcoholism, as a relative, friend or professional, is it is always accompanied by a phenomenon known as denial. In the long path the alcoholic takes toward mental, physical and moral decline, usually the first thing to go is honesty.[94]

I immediately hired a lawyer and a court order was put into place. I was permitted to print the publication using the same name. I was traumatized by this event and I could not fathom how Herald and my ex-friends and employees could live with themselves after doing what they had done. But I had to keep reminding myself that alcoholism, addiction and greed makes people do things they normally would not do. I knew that from personal experience during my drinking days.

Chapter 25
Lies and Deceit

The worst part of the company split was that Herald and some of the ex-employees told many of the clients I was an alcoholic and drug addict. They failed to inform the clients I had been sober and clean for nearly ten years. One worried client called me and wanted to know if I was alright. Herald had told them I had been put in a mental institution, and he did not know when I would be back. Technically, I had been put in a mental institution called rehab, but it was ten years earlier and I had been back for quite along time.

As time went on, their antics and the low levels that they stooped never ceased to amaze me. In retrospect, I choose to believe that many of their tricks to discredit me were instigated by Herald and several of the ex-employees knew nothing about them. Two of the ex-employees called me after working for Herald for about a month and apologized for everything that had happened. They realized what they did was indescribably vicious and they were sorry for their actions. They quit working for him.

Within a short period, the final court orders came through and everything involving the company was completely mine. Like a typical practicing alcoholic, when Herald realized he was losing everything with the company he tried back stepping his actions and requested part of it back. The judge knew his deceptions involving the case and refused his requests. He even tried telling the judge that he did not have anything to do with what happened and the employees had instigated everything on their own. The fact their offices were in a building co-owned by Herald completely discredited his story.

I had a realization that before my sobriety, my past addictions and actions had been as abusive to my family as these people had been to me. The lies and deceit came easily for me when I was drinking and using drugs. When millions of dollars are added to the equation then Herald and the other addict ex-employees' actions were sadly very sick, and part of the addiction disease.

Tony, my friends from my support group, and myself continued running the publication. After all the chaos, the paper continued to do well and we only lost a small percentage of our regular advertisers after all the chaos subsided. This chaos of the alcoholics and addicts were in my life reminded me where I came from. I knew I had to start taking my sobriety seriously again if I wanted to stay sober and sane so I started going to more meetings and joined another women's support group. The worry and the pandemonium surrounding the company for so many months had taken a toll on me. I was depressed and I felt tired and worn all the time.

Depression will be the second largest killer after heart disease by 2020.[95]

The publication had been well known in the adult industry for many years, but after the press coverage of the split we were now known by many outside the industry. After the company divided, I started to have second thoughts about my future. I felt that I should have been doing something more productive and that it was time to move on. However, I did not leave the company until several years later.

I had been together with Tony for many years and he wanted to get married and have children. Having children at that stage of my life would have been a disaster. I was struggling with my depression and I was completely focused on the company. Sadly, Tony and I broke up and we each went our separate ways.

Later, it was not a shock to discover my ex-partner, Herald, had died. He had been floating in his pool dead for a couple of days before someone found him. He had a heart attack and fell over and died in his pool. He was only in his early 40s. The drinking and cocaine had finally caught up with him and he had partied himself to death. All I could think about was not what he had done to himself but the effect this would have on his wife and kids.

My company was going through the motions of printing, sponsoring events and continuing to grow in popularity. I also met a wonderful man, Andy, who eventually came and joined the company. He was very sweet and spoiled me immensely. The first year we were dating he sent me roses every week. Andy knew how to win me over and I loved every second of his pampering.

I met Andy at a party with my sober friends. He was also in recovery and had been clean and sober for about 5 years. Andy was handsome, funny and attentive and had just moved back to Dallas. He did not have many friends so we spent a lot of time together. We went to meetings together and went out with our sober friends frequently. After a short period of time, Andy moved into my house with me and eventually came to work for my company. He treated my mother like she was his own and he quickly became a part of my family.

The beginning of our relationship was like a dream, and we were married. But sometimes you wake up and the fantasy is over.

Chapter 26
Letting Go of Pride & Ego

After the catastrophe of 9/11, the advertising business hit bottom. The entertainment business slacked off because everyone feared going out and the advertising dropped like a steel trap closing shut. Since the ads were not plentiful that meant that the money was not either. Andy and I were under a lot of pressure to pay the printing costs and meet the employees' payroll.

Stress was at an all time high and I already wanted to sell the accounts and start something new. I was dealing with my depression and not in the best frame of mind when I started noticing drastic changes in Andy's behaviors. At first, I thought I was overreacting, but then I realized Andy's personality change was not my imagination when employees came to me concerned about his behaviors. He was getting hostile and losing his temper at home and in the office. I thought the stress of the business was getting to him and he needed to relax and take some time off. However, he rejected this idea and insisted he was fine.

Only 8% of the approximately 22 million Americans aged 12 and older who need addiction care receive treatment for their disorder.[96]

It did not take me long to discover Andy had started drinking again. I found cases of beer hidden in the garage. I was amazed I had not considered he had started drinking. The alcohol explained his behavior and personality changes, his anger and hostility. Alcoholics can be the most wonderful people when we are sober, but give us a drink and we turn into a fire-breathing monster on a path of destruction.

When I confronted Andy about his drinking he was forced to admit he had started again. He had no remorse or regret and declared he was really not an alcoholic and he could drink if he desired. I knew that Andy's denial was back in full-force when he insisted he was not like "those" people at recovery meetings and he refused to go. I was crushed and concerned about Andy because he was drinking and driving. I was afraid he would kill himself or someone else. He already had numerous DWIs (not all on his record) and he had been in a horrific accident which broke his back while drinking and driving. In fact, he had titanium rods holding his spine in place.

I knew I could not live with someone who was drinking with serious anger issues. I had never witnessed someone go so quickly into denial as he had. Many of the people I had been exposed to would admit to having a "slip" (drank or used drugs again) and often they would come back into the program. I had never heard any of them deny, even when they were drinking they were alcoholics. Andy was adamant he was not an alcoholic and I knew the man I first met and loved was gone.

This was my chance to get out of the company and end the relationship at the same time. Andy wanted to take over the company and I wanted out, so that is what we arranged. After a few short months, I left the company I had poured myself into for many years. I had founded, created, established and watched it have ups and downs. It was a very difficult decision, but I was no longer happy and needed to leave.

After I left, I contemplated why I had kept the company for so many years when I was not happy working there. I unveiled my true self and realized that my ego and pride had stopped me. I liked people knowing me and I liked everyone knowing I built a successful company. The cars, the house, the expensive material possessions were also fun to have. I think Dudley Moore in the movie "Arthur" summed it up perfectly, "Being rich doesn't suck."

Finally, I had set my pride and ego aside and left… it was the best decision I had made for myself in a decade. I had no idea what I was going to do and I knew I had to take some time off to focus on myself and my sobriety. A beautiful lady, Audrey, who was a faithful member of Alanon, opened her home to me. I moved in with her and started a new phase of my life. She understood the perils of alcoholism and drug addiction whole heartedly. She had lost her husband to suicide because of his alcoholism. Audrey was very active in Alanon and encouraged me to start going to meetings with her and join her support group. It was exactly what I needed and the group reinforced the truth. Andy's drinking and behaviors had nothing to do with me and I could do nothing to help him at this stage of his disease. Once again, I felt the unconditional love and caring from this new recovery group. Even though most were not alcoholics or drug addicts themselves, they had experienced living and dealing with alcoholism throughout their lives. They had suffered and endured an alcoholic in their lives like I had my father's alcoholism.

While I was living with Audrey, I was in a safe environment that allowed me to focus on taking care of myself. The stress had been removed and now it was time to focus on the basics of recovery again and spend time alone with my Higher Power. At 35 years, I felt old and tired and my body physically and mentally needed to rest.

Chapter 27
Life Changing Events

After several months, I started to think about my future and what I wanted to do. I knew it was time to give back and to be of service to others. Recovery groups teach this and finally after many years of sobriety I was beginning to understand the importance of this concept.

I had briefly taught night school at one of the universities, and I wanted to teach again. It was my first passion that I did not pursue when I was drinking and drugging. I decided I wanted to teach high school, preferably in an economically disadvantaged area of Dallas. After about eight months of rest and relaxation at Audrey's, I got a job in exactly the type of high school I desired. I knew teaching in an inner city high school would be a challenge, but I was ready for my new adventure.

Once I started getting to know the students at school and being a part of their lives it completely changed mine. I have never felt like I was making a real difference in other people's lives until now. When my students give me a quick hug, my heart melts and it is filled with love.

In recovery, they say you will lose your selfishness and become concerned about others. After many years of sobriety, this finally happened to me. Being an active part of community service changes a person's perception of what is important in life. My depression has disappeared and I have the experience and true feelings of being happy, joyous and free.

My mom and I became close friends during my sobriety and were very active in each others lives, especially after I began teaching. Years ago, I never thought that I would ever grow to truly love her, but because of the recovery process I was able to let go of the past and start fresh with our relationship. At 79 years old, she still worked part time and had an incredible social life. I was proud of her for becoming her own woman after my father's death. I believe that Alanon, and her friends in the program helped her grow and find herself.

It took me several years after my divorce to start dating anyone seriously, but I finally did. I started dating a "normie" whose idea of drinking was having a beer or two a couple of times a month. I have never understood why someone would want to have only a couple of drinks.

I always wondered, "Why bother?" I am still perplexed when someone leaves an alcoholic beverage unfinished. It's just another confirmation that I truly am an alcoholic.

My new boyfriend, Bradley, and I had the same interests and hobbies: we rode motorcycles together, we watched football, he was a pilot and we flew on short trips. Most importantly, we enjoyed each others company. We would see each other a few times a week and had our separate lives and friends. He taught me how to date and have a healthy relationship without smothering each other. Bradley became one of my closest friends and we dated for almost three years. I yearned for the relationship to progress and he did not. I was extremely upset when we parted ways, but I knew from all my codependency treatment and experiences I was going to be alright on my own. I did not feel the overwhelming sensation I would die if we were not together. I was heartbroken and miserable, but recovery had taught me to love myself and be comfortable as a single woman. I knew I did not need a man to survive and thrive. We are both friends to this day and I value and love his dear friendship.

A few months after Bradley's and our breakup, without warning, my mom had a heart attack and died. Thankfully, I was there and took her to the hospital when she first started showing symptoms. Within 24 hours of being admitted, she passed on. My sister, my close friend Cindi, and I were blessed to be with her during her final moments. Being able to be there for her was an incredible gift not only for my mother but also for me. Also, having such a loving and caring sister and friend by her side was a blessing that will never be forgotten.

I felt like I had lost two of my closest friends. My mother was gone and Bradley was not a part of my daily life any longer. I could not imagine my life without one of them and having the absence of both of them was painfully challenging. Once again, my support group and my friends were there for support and comfort. I can not imagine my life today without being clean and sober, having my friends, and being in recovery.

The meeting time is coming to a close. Thank you for asking me to tell my story tonight, I never want to forget where I came from and how far I have come in sobriety.

Let me end by sharing one of my favorite quotes, '*Take the first step in faith. You don't have to see the whole staircase. Just take the first step.*' That is a quote from the late, great Martin Luther King, Jr."

The meeting ends and my past has been exposed. The other recovering alcoholics and addicts give me a warm round of applause and smiles. There is a strong bond between us. We have journeys with similar experiences, thoughts and feelings that have led us all to recovery and for that I am truly grateful.

Section II

Chapters 28–31
Sobriety Suggestions

"Happiness and freedom begin with a clear understanding of one principle: some things are within our control and some things are not. It is only after you have faced up to this fundamental rule and learned to distinguish between what you can and cannot control that inner tranquility and outer effectiveness become possible."

– Epicetus, Stoic Philosopher (In approx. 95 AD.)

Chapter 28
High Spirits

Making the decision to get clean and sober was the biggest life-changing event and blessing of my life. Remaining clean and sober is my first priority today. I know if I am not clean and sober, I am not of service to anyone… including myself. I have accepted the fact I have a progressive disease called alcoholism and I am a drug addict. Even though I have not had a drink or drug since 1988 does not mean the disease has disappeared. In fact, since the disease is a progressive disease; if I were to start using and drinking again I would immediately be right back where I left off. Sadly, I have witnessed this repeatedly with friends who have been sober and had "slips." My fear is if I drink or drug again I would end up like many who do not make it back to their support group and eventually die.

A slow gradual death from alcoholism is something I desire to avoid at all lengths. As my story exhibits, getting clean and sober was not a fast, easy process for me. I did not see any burning bushes that miraculously changed my life instantaneously. It was a slow process with gradual changes in my attitudes and personality. The program taught me to find *my own* Higher Power who has filled my life with countless blessings for which I am exceedingly grateful.

Not only has the desire to drink and drug been lifted today, but the severe depressions that once ruled my life have vanished. I believe in myself today and have self-confidence I never thought possible. The support groups, my Higher Power, positive affirmations, my friends and family, have all contributed to saving my life.

Today, I can honestly say I am eternally grateful for my support groups and their programs and all the recovering alcoholics who have touched my life over the years. The encouragement, concern and unconditional love offered freely has done exactly what Sammy said would happen 18 years earlier…. I was *"Loved Back to Life."*

Chapter 29
Motorcycle Therapy

I started riding motorcycles and trikes (3 wheel motorcycles), after my first few years of sobriety. Riding helped me learn how to have fun without alcohol and drugs. There's no experience more rejuvenating when you are riding down the street on a motorcycle with the wind in your face and feeling a sense of freedom. Often, when I am feeling low and having a bad day, I will jump on my hot pink cycle, start the engine and the moment I hit the throttle I feel invigorated.

There are many sober motorcycle enthusiasts in the program who ride together and who over the years have become my true friends. They have made my weekends incredibly fun and adventurous and the most amazing part is we are all in recovery.

Many consider riding motorcycles a lifestyle; I agree with this sentiment. Staying sober and being in recovery is also a lifestyle and if you put the two together, you have found a way of life you will cherish.

Sober riders often joke, "Get a year of sobriety under your belt, buy a motorcycle, ride with sober friends, and you won't think about drinking or drugging."

Many years ago, at one of the motorcycle rallies, I was given a card from the Christian Motorcycle Association and I have kept it hanging on my refrigerator ever since. No matter what name you associate with your Higher Power you can appreciate what it says:

"He Would Have Ridden A Harley: Jesus the Biker"
He was a lot like you and me.
The government didn't like him.
The church thought he was weird.
His friends were few.
What friends he had, denied him.
He was persecuted by hypocrites.
He hung around people like you and me, not the goody-two-shoes Pharisees.
Riding two wheels moves a person's soul to a new height of
personal freedom of the mind, body and spirit.

Chapter 30
Positive Power of Suggesting

This chapter is designed to give suggestions to those who are striving for sobriety. These are factors that positively affected my sobriety and helped me to stay sober, grow as a person and find my own spirituality. *Remember - not everything works for everybody and we all have to find our own road to recovery.* My hope is some of these suggestions will help others find their way.

It's only for a day.

You often hear in recovery groups all you have to do is stay sober "one day at a time." I know when I was first getting sober I could not fathom not drinking or drugging for the rest of my life. But if I thought of not drinking or drugging for one 24 hour period then I thought maybe it was possible. Sometimes even 24 hours seemed like a long time and I would have to stay sober one hour at a time and even one minute at a time and I knew I could definitely do that.

The hours eventually led to days and the days led to weeks and the weeks led to months and the months led to years. Eventually not picking up a drink or drug became easier. The obsession occupied my thoughts less by going to meetings and keeping close to my sober friends. Over time, the obsession to drink faded until it was gone.

Consider treatment and counseling.

I was fortunate to have insurance covering most of my treatment in the rehabilitation center at the hospital. I personally think it is important to get professional help and treatment when possible. Many alcoholics and addicts (including myself) have other mental and emotional issues needing to be dealt with immediately. Leaving a mentally ill person who is depressed untreated especially while they are trying to get sober, is a disaster waiting to happen. There is no shame in getting the proper help and it does not make a person weak. It's quite the opposite, once a person goes to treatment or counseling they become strong while the weak ones who did not have the courage to ask for help usually do not stay sober and do not get well.

Even if you do not have insurance there are many facilities free to those in need. If you ask enough people, you will find the help available.

Of course, not every alcoholic and addict needs rehabilitation, treatment or counseling. There are many who do not have other mental illnesses and can get sober and clean and lead happy, healthy lives by finding the right recovery group and being active in the program.

Medication

I am not a medical doctor, so I can only share my experience with you about medication. I found that it was necessary for me to take anti-depressants. Often alcoholics and addicts (especially women) suffer from severe depression and can not function without the help of medication. If a doctor suggests that you may have a disorder and suggests medication, then take the doctor's advice to heart and take the medication. Do not turn down the medication because you are alcohol and drug free. If your body needs help to stay mentally balanced then take the meds. If you were a diabetic and were getting clean and sober you would not refuse to take your insulin. It's the same principal with anti-depressants, if you need them to get and stay well because your body is not producing the chemicals necessary to stay balanced then listen to your doctor.

If I had not taken anti-depressants then I may not be alive today. They helped me pull myself out of the gutter of depression after I had destroyed parts of my brain using hardcore illegal drugs. As a result, the chemicals were not being produced properly in my brain and I was like a limp noodle lying around. Anti-depressants are not "miracle pills" and will not make you instantly happy. But from my experience a person can remain clean and sober, take the meds as prescribed by the doctor and find true happiness.

If you are on medication and someone in the program tells you to stop taking them then talk to someone else who has had the same experience you are going through. I highly suggest you do not stop taking your medication because of someone in the program who does not understand your problem's full scope. This does not happen very often, but every once in a while it does and it concerns me deeply. I know without my medication I would not have been able to conquer my depression and I would have killed myself. There is not a doubt in my mind this is where I was headed before I started taking my medication and going to therapy even though I was not drinking and drugging. My body was not physically capable of healing itself without medication.

I have heard the story of a lady in a recovery program who was sponsoring a newly sober woman. This woman told her sponsor that she suffered from depression and could barely get out of bed in the morning. The newcomer was actually bi-polar and was very normal when she took the medication. However, off the medicine she was completely insane with a vivid imagination that ran wild. She believed people were after her and would disappear for days and weeks at a time hiding. On her medication she was happy, healthy and a great employee, but when she did not take her medication she ended up living in her car begging for money and food. This newcomer wanted more than anything to stay clean and sober and listened to her sponsor and got off her bi-polar medication. She ended up losing all her senses and killing herself one night. My advice is to listen to your doctor and take medication if necessary.

Do alcoholics always stay sober the first time they try?

I watched people who were having problems staying sober come and go, in and out of the program. Many of these people did not make it back from their "slips." Some died from suicide, alcohol consumption and over dosing on drugs. My fear was - and still is - I would end up living in the vivacious circle of alcoholism and develop a wet brain.

A friend of mine with many years of sobriety and who has sponsored many men suddenly started drinking again. Once he began drinking he was off to the races. Even after all those years of sobriety, he picked up right where he left off. All his friends were distraught as we watched his disease take over him. He went from being a very handsome man, having a wonderful life with many friends, owning a beautiful home, working a great job and being everything one could desire, to living on the streets under a bridge within a very short period of time.

I did not know that he was homeless until one day when I was driving to work downtown and I saw him first hand. There was the man I cared about deeply, who helped me get sober, who had been a respected man in his community, standing on the street corner begging for money. He was barely recognizable, he had lost his teeth, he was in dirty torn clothes and he was as thin as a rail. His once sparkling blue eyes that I had admired so much were now dull and dark.

I truly feared after witnessing some of my friends who started drinking and drugging after being in sobriety that if I "slipped" that I would not have another sobering up. An alcoholic and an addict never knows what will happen when they take that first drink or drug.

Of course, some people come and go from recovery groups and only accumulate small stints of being sober. However, those who continue going back to meetings often end up with long term sobriety. Every alcoholic and addict has their own path that they individually have to follow.

Remember your feelings when first getting sober.

I do not and have not forgotten the feelings of emotional chaos and inner turmoil overwhelming me before and during treatment. The horrendous feelings of depression and pain consuming every cell in my body will always remain in my mind. The deep, dark pit of despair in my soul that I called the "black hole" was so empty and agonizing has finally disappeared and is no longer a part of me, but I remember how it felt. Remembering the struggle of the mental and physical all-encompassing obsession to drink and drug has always been a key to my personal recovery.

Even though I have not forgotten these past feelings, I have long let go of them so I was able to move on in my sobriety.

Find your own personal Higher Power.

Before entering a recovery group I feared God and thought I was doomed for a miserable life and after-life. I believed God thought I was an appalling person because of all the terrible things I had done in my past. At that time, I thought that God hated me and did not care.

I had to learn to let go of my old damning beliefs and get to know a new God that loved me, cared about me, understood me, believed in me and most importantly forgave me for my past misdeeds. Getting to know a new God of my understanding and discarding my old belief system was a slow process. But I listened and learned about other sober alcoholics' Higher Powers and eventually found mine.

Once I started having faith in a caring, loving God who wanted what was best for me then I began to change from the inside out. I began believing in myself and relying on my Higher Power more and more.

Many people who come into the program do not have a perception of their Higher Powers and there are many names associated with God.

Do not let the name I have for my Higher Power discourage you from entering a support group. Once in the program, you will find that it does not matter what you call your Higher Power or even if you do not have one. Everything comes in time.

Miracles start happening.

Throughout my recovery, especially in the beginning, I would start having doubts about my sobriety because I could not see the changes in myself. I was encouraged to watch others and focus on how they were changing. I saw other people's fear and anger disappear and the people who once cared only about themselves began helping others in the program. I watched people relying on their personal faith for jobs, family situations and financial frustrations. They were changing before my eyes. It was easier to see changes in friends than changes happening within myself. Even when I could not see changes in myself, by watching others in recovery I gained confidence that I could also change.

Read program related materials and self-help books.

I had to focus my entire mind, heart and soul into recovery. For many years my friends and the program filled all my time away from work. I knew my untreated alcoholic way of thinking was warped and I had to retrain my mind and get a different attitude if I wanted to remain sober. The only way I knew how to do that was to attend a lot of meetings and read a lot of books.

Every recovery program has their own book they abide by. The "Big Book" of Alcoholics Anonymous was the first recovery book written using the 12 steps in the 1930s. Most of the other recovery books published since then have been modeled after this book including Narcotics Anonymous, Cocaine Anonymous, etc. I studied my recovery books relentlessly.

These books became my security blankets. I would read them repeatedly, but it did not start sinking in until I started studying the information relentlessly. While I studied I would highlight my favorite parts and put dates next to the parts that enlightened me for that day. I went to book studies and listened. I participated in the reading and added to the discussions. I desired to understand as much of the books as possible because I surmised if I learned as much as I could then I would learn more about alcoholism, addiction and myself.

There are numerous other books written on alcoholism and co-dependency that I have read several times and helped me significantly. *New Pair of Glasses* by Chuck C is a must read for anyone getting clean and sober. Since I was also dealing with co-dependency issues, I read and highly recommend two books. One suggestion is *Boundaries, Where You End and I Begin* by Anne Katherine and another is *Co-dependency No More* by Melody Beattie. Both of these authors have several other books that are very beneficial to recovery. These books taught me more about separating myself from the chaos and others. I learned I am my own person and I do not need to rely on anyone else for my happiness. I was not the reason for another persons actions and I could not control others behaviors...only my own.

Learn to meditate.

Everyone meditates or prays differently. Some people pray as a way to meditate and some meditate as a way to pray. Just like we all have to find our own personal Higher Power, we need to learn to meditate and pray in our own way. For me, my meditation and prayers are usually separate, but sometimes they do overlap. I use meditation to relax myself, to be calm and erase my thoughts. Sometimes I will listen to soft, mellow music and other times I prefer silence. I sit comfortably and try to clear my head by relaxing my muscles. I have no set time frame for my meditating. Sometimes it is long and sometimes it is short. Meditation was also a process for me and was not something I was able to instantly accomplish when I quit drinking. Even now, some days my thoughts spin. Trying to stop the party going on in my head is either very difficult or impossible. When that happens, I try again later when my mind is not off on a tangent.

Practice Positive Affirmations.

I believe that positive affirmations have largely contributed to my depression lifting and my negative attitude dissolving away. I repeat positive affirmations to myself at least twice a day. I spend anywhere from 15 to 30 minutes saying positive affirmations out loud to myself. My favorite place to do my affirmations is when I am driving my car. I also enjoy saying the affirmations when I am in the shower or in the bathtub relaxing. Sometimes I am not in a place to say them out loud so I repeat them to myself silently.

My positive affirmations consist of saying uplifting, productive things about myself. By repeating these affirmations over and over again, I came to see the positive aspects of myself. I gained confidence and now believe and know I will succeed in achieving all my dreams and goals.

I keep my affirmations short, sweet and to the point. For example, I repeat the following: *I am happy, joyous and free; I am loved; I am loving; I am kind; I am trustworthy; I am honest; I am fun; I am prosperous; I am successful,* etc. Once I start saying my affirmations, I add on to the list when I desire and I often repeat the same ones over and over again. There are free positive affirmations listed on our website www.lovedbacktolife.com. Print them out and put them in a place where you can read them in the morning and have a copy available to read during the day when your attitude needs a "Positive Pick-Up."

My favorite book for becoming aware of what we are all capable of achieving and for positive uplifting affirmations is *The Secret* by Rhonda Byrne. I have learned to concentrate on the positives in life. When we have faith in our Higher Power and ourselves anything is possible. When I meditate I focus on the positive, all the things I am grateful for and the person I want to become. This action has made phenomenal differences in my attitude and my quality of sobriety. It has made my dream of becoming an author who helps millions of people become educated on alcoholism and drug addiction come to fusion.

My experience has been that when I started being optimistic then all areas of my life became prosperous. Positive affirmations always help when I am feeling depressed. Even on those days when it sometimes may seem easier not to wander far from bed I find the energy to say my affirmations. Today, I believe the truth of the affirmations I tell myself…I am a wonderful, successful, and loving person.

Learn to pray.

Since I had my strict religious upbringing, I had been taught to pray in church. But, I did not want to pray when I started in recovery because my perception of my Higher Power still had a negative connotation. My sponsor encouraged me to pray even if I did not want to… so I did. I prayed even when I thought it was a charade, and eventually my perceptions changed. I began truly meaning and feeling my prayers. Sometimes newcomers do not have any perception of a Higher Power and they prayed because they believed that others believed. When I prayed I was told to ask for His guidance, protection and to stay alcohol and drug free and that is exactly what I did. If I was not sober I had nothing.

Today, I pray and "talk to God" throughout the day. I ask for help in situations or sometimes I need to calm down and regroup so I say a quick prayer to get me back on track. I talk to God like he is my friend and confidant. This is a far cry from once believing I was going to descend into the fury of hell.

I am always seeking new sources to improve myself, my meditations, positive affirmations and prayers. I found the book called *The Prayer of Jabez* and its' *31 day devotional* by Bruce Wilkinson brought me closer to my Higher Power. It contributed to me finding more confidence in my connection with God and reiterated that many of my old ideas I had negatively perceived as a child were untrue. I recommend this book to anyone who is struggling and coming to terms with a past concept of God as unforgiving and damning. It reinforces my God is loving and caring and wants what is best for me.

Journal at night.

When I crawl into bed at night I take my pen and pad and write about my day. It is important for me to review my actions and attitudes. My journal mostly consists of my feelings. I write if I am happy, sad, angry, embarrassed, or ashamed and I list all the feelings I had throughout the day. I do not want to stuff feelings like I did for nearly two decades. I want to keep my inner self from exploding with raging negative emotions again.

By journaling, I can also see where I need to make changes in my behavior and where I could have handled circumstances better. If I feel like I need to apologize to someone, I can look at the situation and prepare myself for the amends.

Sober people become new friends.

New friends in the program replaced my using and drinking friends. I knew I had to let go of the friends that I partied with if I was going to remain sober. I had to release my old life and make a new one if I was going to heal physically and emotionally. During my first year of sobriety, I rarely went places where alcohol would be prevalent. I did not want to put my sobriety in jeopardy and it was very important for me to feel like I was in a safe supportive environment.

After a couple of years of sobriety, I started going to concerts and dance clubs again with sober friends. However, I always drove my own car wherever I was going incase I felt uncomfortable so I could immediately leave.

Call a sober person to talk.

Sometimes a person just has a bad day. Things are not going well and you are frustrated. Every once in a while you need to make a decision and you need to talk to a sober friend first to sort out your thoughts. This was a new concept for me because I rarely talked about my feelings to anyone. I was always afraid to tell someone my thoughts because I knew I did not think sanely at times. But I did learn to pick up the phone and call someone and they would put my feelings and thoughts in perspective for me. They would listen and make suggestions and I would feel better. Often just venting about a problem releases all the frustration. Talking and purging my feelings did not come naturally for me. For so many years, I had held everything I thought and felt inside myself. At first, I was embarrassed and reluctant to share with another person. Once I started sharing with another person, I realized that it was much easier than hiding my true self.

There were many times when I would air my feelings to a friend's voice mail just to vent. Email is another great tool to use for expressing your emotions. I would type out a short (sometimes lengthy) email to a friend to rid myself of my aggravations. However, if you are angry do NOT shoot off an email you will regret later to the person whom your anger is directed. If you type an email to someone you are angry with then I suggest you send it to another friend and not the person you are upset with.

In the beginning, all that I knew was I could not keep my ill feelings bottled up inside me, if I was to stay sober so I released them any way possible. When I was first getting sober, I had so much anger and hostility in my personality that it was progress for me if I did not have a raging episode for a few days. Over time, by staying sober and learning to control my, anger the incidents became further and further apart and now they rarely occur.

Go to less fortunate places where people are trying to get sober.

One of the best ways to get myself out of my own head is to go to less fortunate places where people were trying to stay sober. There are meetings in hospitals, rehabs, half-way houses, the Salvation Army, and the inner city. When I am feeling sorry for myself, I go to places where the people are far less fortunate and need help. Talking to other alcoholics and addicts with no job, no money, and no place to sleep always puts a different perceptive on my life. They are alcoholics and drug addicts with the exact same progressive disease I have. We have a common bond bringing understanding and caring. They have lost everything in their lives and miraculously their primary focus is not drinking or drugging. They realize, like I do, without sobriety we do not have a chance.

When I go to these meetings it causes what I like to call "Instantaneous Gratitude." It is impossible to leave without being grateful for my sobriety and all of my gifts and blessings. It also gives me a sense of being of assistance for another brother and/or sister alcoholic addict and that is what the basis of sobriety is all about.

Different alcoholics and drug addicts have different bottoms. Some lose everything and only have the clothes on their backs, while others drive to meetings in expensive cars and live in fancy houses. It does not matter what we have in material possessions when we first get sober, what matters is we all feel the same horrendous pain. Our lives have come to dead end, and we have no where else to go.

Learn to identify and not to compare.

Instead of looking for differences between myself and the people at meetings, I learned to stop comparing myself and start identifying with our likenesses. It is much easier to find differences in others because we look different and are different ages, genders, religions, races, educational and income levels. When I started to pay attention to the similarities in being alcoholics and drug addicts I began to relate to others. When I listened, I heard we all had the same damaged thoughts and an overwhelming amount of similar feelings and fears. We experienced the same drunken stupors and could not live in our own skins any longer before striving for sobriety. Once the outside physical factors are cast aside, every alcoholic and addict has the same immense sense of failure and ache when they decide to get help.

Listen to people with long-term sobriety.

I realized people with long-term sobriety (also known as Oldtimers) had a lot more experience staying sober and I could not imagine not having a drink for as long as they had abstained. I may not have liked some of their personalities, but they knew how to stay sober and I listened to them. All I wanted to do was to stay sober under any circumstance and when they told me to make coffee or clean the mugs and the ashtrays (even though I did not smoke), I did it. I vacuumed floors, washed windows, cleaned bathrooms, and emptied the trash. They told me I needed to be of service to others and I did what they suggested. I probably would have walked on my hands through broken glass when I was struggling to stay sober if it would have helped me from not drinking and drugging.

Listen during meetings.

At first, I had a difficult time sitting still through an hour long meeting. I would be distracted easily, I would wave at whoever came in late, leave to go to the restroom, get a soda and do anything so I did not have to sit and pay attention to what was being said.

An "Oldtimer" told me I needed to sit still and listen to what others were sharing or I would not stay sober. She suggested if I was not able to sit still without my mind wandering then I needed to sit on my hands and stare at the ground. She said it was not necessary for me to look up unless I was called on. Furthermore, I should not leave my seat for any reason. This way I could not be distracted. I could concentrate and focus on what was being said during the meeting. Her suggestion worked. As I sat on my hands and stared at the floor through meetings I started hearing and relating to what was happening during the meetings. I am happy to say that over time, I was able to sit through meetings and have free use of my hands.

Let go of the past.

Letting go of the past was a process for me. It would have been great if I woke up one day and everything that I despised about my drinking days just disappeared magically. But it took time before I was able to release myself of my past discrepancies. I had to begin believing that my Higher Power was forgiving. Also, it was a necessity that I learn to forgive myself. This was a new concept for me. I had to accept the responsibility of my actions, attitudes and behaviors in the past and accept being an alcoholic was also forgivable. I had to accept being an alcoholic was not my fault, but my choices I made while drinking and drugging were my responsibility. Overtime, I was able to forgive myself and know my Higher Power has forgiven me also.

Chapter 31
The Big "Do Nots" of Recovery (Easier Said Than Done)

The following is a list of the "Do Nots" that I suggest for someone in recovery. Of course, every alcoholic and addict is unique and not everything works for everybody. As I stated earlier, I was not a recovery "Honor Student." I chose to experience some of the "Do Nots" in my sobriety. We each have our own path, but these "Do Nots" are some of the most prevalent mistakes that often put alcoholics' sobriety in jeopardy. By avoiding these blunders, it could possibly make life easier in sobriety.

Do not forget to become friends with people of the same gender.

There are meetings that are for women only and for men only. I was never comfortable with groups of women when I first got sober and, as a result, I shied away from women's meetings. But once I got up the nerve to try it, the closeness and companionship the women offered was irreplaceable. It was often said if I wanted to stay sober to stick with the women. I have women friends that I have known for nearly 20 years who have witnessed all my ups and downs and sobriety. They have always been there for me and no matter what choices I made (good and bad) they always supported me. Before sobriety, I always put myself first and my friends needs far behind mine. But a true gift of sobriety is being able to reciprocate and learn how to be a true loving friend.

Do not put anyone on a pedestal.

For many years in sobriety, I made the mistake of putting friends, sponsors and "Oldtimers" on pedestals. I thought they were gurus and could do no wrong. The problem with that theory is that we are all human with faults and everyone will disappoint periodically. I had unrealistic expectations of certain people. No one is perfect and I was expecting sobriety to make everyone perfect. Obviously, that is an impossible feat for anyone and I was often disappointed because we all have imperfections.

Recovery does not make us flawless. Instead it lets us grow and progress toward our ultimate goals.

Do not have unrealistic expectations.

I believe we can be our own worst enemy. Alcoholics and addicts tend to "beat ourselves up" when we make mistakes. Once I started on the road of recovery and had been sober for awhile it seems I became harder on myself. Because I was sober, I expected all of my character defects would automatically be fixed. Time and again, I thought I should not be making mistakes, getting angry or having resentments. I should handle all situations correctly and flawlessly. It is just like having to stop the delusions that other people are perfect, I had the same unrealistic expectations about myself. Do not believe just because a person stops drinking and drugging their life and behaviors will instantly be ideal.

The objective of recovery is to stay clean and sober. Over time our character defects will change if a person sticks close to their support group. This process does not happen rapidly. In recovery I had to learn how to live without alcohol and drugs and how to act and react in sobriety. So, at first, do not have too high expectations. Change will come as one grows spiritually and gets to know them self better.

Do not stop going to your support group.

Sometimes, if someone upset me or I had a disagreement with someone at my support group, I would stop going. I would wait until things blew over or until I was not as angry and resentful as I had been. Then I would go back to meetings. I was taking the chance I could possibly drink over a stupid situation because I was distancing myself from my recovery group.

The worst time to stop going to meetings is when an alcoholic is angry. Alcoholics will drink when their anger flares. Avoidance for alcoholics can be deadly. Talk to another sober friend or work the problem out. Until then, stick with your support group. Focus on the reason you have the support group…to stay sober. Everything else is happening needs to be set aside so we do not loose track of what is important…not taking that first drink or drug.

Do not get hung up on your past.

This was touched on in the other section called "Let Go of Your Past." However, it is extremely important aspect of my sobriety so I feel I need to share more on the topic.

We all enter into recovery with different pasts. Many of us come from dysfunctional homes where a parent may have been an alcoholic and/or was abusive. Some were physically abused, neglected, abandoned, overly protected and/or sexually abused. Granted, not all alcoholics have these experiences, but many do. When some one has experienced repeated emotional or physical abuse it may be more difficult to let go of the past. This may sound strange to a person who has not had these types of experiences. You probably are thinking, "Why wouldn't abused people let go of the past quickly and get on with their lives?" It is not that simple. Once an experience has been ingrained in a person it becomes a part of them. Letting go, even of negative situations is a very difficult process.

For example, I had a difficult time remembering a lot of my childhood. As a defense mechanism, often our minds block out the emotionally destructive times. It is a survival mechanism. When I was growing up it was easier to put the abuse out of my mind because it was too painful to hold on to. The only way I could cope was to stuff the memory and try to forget. Because I could not remember everything, I thought I could not get better. This is not true. I learned I can let go of the past I remembered, as well as what has been blocked from my memory. If I am suppose to remember more from my childhood then it will be revealed in time. If not, that is alright too.

Another example of not remembering was when I went into blackouts from drinking or raging. When I was drinking I would blackout and still function normally to other people. I would have no idea what had happened when I woke up the next day. My raging blackouts were similar. I would get to a point where I passed the anger stage and crossed into a raging fit. Once I reached that level, I could not remember what I said or did. But whatever I did during my blackouts I needed to release from my past. No matter what it was, I had to forgive myself.

Do not stop doing what to makes you feel good.

Sometimes when I began to feel better because I was in a routine of going to my support group, meditating and praying, I would slack off and stop doing them daily. Somewhere in my alcoholic twisted head I would convince myself I felt better so I did not have to stick to my routine anymore. Once I started slacking off with the important factors of my sobriety then I would start feeling disenchanted. I will never understand why alcoholics and addicts (including myself) who begin to feel more spiritually connected and healthier than ever then stop practicing what they know is making the difference. However, it is very common.

Exercise and working out regularly is another prime example. Even non-alcoholics start working out, lose weight, start feeling better and then slack off. They get out of their routine until they stop exercising all together and gain their weight back.

It is extremely important to stay with a routine that makes you feel better. It is easy to become content and comfortable with your alcoholism in recovery, but that is when you are giving the "Old Denial Beast" a chance to raise his ugly head again. Once denial takes over, drinking is the next step. There is no guarantee the drunk (formerly sober alcoholic) will ever find recovery again.

Do not get involved with the drama of others.

It is so easy to focus on other peoples' problems and how you can help fix them…at least for me it was. So often, co-dependency goes hand in hand with a person who is recovering from alcoholism. I found myself spotlighting and making other peoples' problems my own. I believe the reason alcoholics in sobriety try to "fix" others' situations is because then we do not have to focus on our own defects.

Of course, it is important to help others in recovery. However, it is essential to remember that we are not capable of "fixing" anyone, anything or any situation. The best way to help others is by living our lives in recovery with our best morals and attitudes. In other words, lead by example.

There are many sober alcoholics and addicts who also join a group for families and friends of alcoholics called Alanon. It is a recovery program that helps persons deal with codependency issues and is also based on a 12 Step program.

Do not date within your support group.

It seems to happen over and over again. People new in sobriety come to a support group and start dating another newcomer or alcoholic.

From my personal experiences, this rarely ends positively. When a person is new in sobriety with twisted thinking and struggling not to drink and drug then starting a relationship with someone feeling the exact same way is not the answer…it *usually* is a disaster.

Often when the relationship goes sour one or both of the alcoholics get drunk again. Although I have seen this situation happen more in early sobriety, it also happens when people have long-term recovery. Relationships and breaking up have a gut-wrenching affect on many sober alcoholics. (This could stem from codependency issues.) However, through my own experiences, if an alcoholic in recovery is determined to stay sober they can as long as they focus on the basics and keep close to other sober friends.

Do not use relationships to fill a void.

Recovering from alcoholism and drug addiction is difficult. When I got sober I had to release the alcohol and drugs attempting to fill the void inside of me for so long. I realized once my vices were gone then the void became deeper and darker than ever. The loneliness and pain is disillusioning. It is common for people in recovery to use relationships with the opposite sex as a way to fill the void.

Relationships take the focus off of ourselves and we focus on our new "love." Sex is an easy way to make ourselves briefly feel better. Many times there are sober alcoholics who jump from one relationship to the next temporarily filling the hollowness. This will not work forever because eventually a person has to learn to fill the emptiness with a Higher Power and by loving one's self.

It is frequently said not to get into a relationship with someone of the opposite sex your first year in recovery. Of course, when a newcomer hears this it seems ludicrous and unfair. But when they are reminded their best thinking got them to where they are today and they need to radically change themselves before they attempt anything new, then it sometimes makes more sense. Also, the longer a person has been sober the clearer reasoning becomes. If newcomers start focusing on someone else and not fully on their recovery it often ends with a drink or a drug. As a newcomer, I was not capable of making any important decisions on my own and relationships always made situations more complicated and difficult. Until a person loves them self a successful relationship is not possible. I suggest taking the time to journey through recovery for awhile before entering the dating scene. Understand what it is like to have friends, be a friend to others, and most importantly to be a friend to yourself.

Do not let depression kill you.

So many alcoholics and addicts suffer from serious depression throughout their lives. My depression started very young and I struggled with it for many years. Just like alcoholism, if you have not experienced depression you can not fully understand this. It invades your body like an evil force and it sometimes stays for long periods of time. Once a person stops drinking and using sometimes their depression becomes more severe.

I learned I could not lay around for days, weeks or months at a time wondering if I would ever feel better. I had to push myself to get up and find help because I could not stand living with such a sense of negativity controlling me. There were many days when it was physically and mentally impossible for me to get out of bed. Eating and taking a shower seemed laborious, but I found the last bit of energy inside myself and found help. No one has to struggle with depression and suicidal thoughts forever. Ask for help even when you feel like it is useless and hopeless…get help from a professional.

I have learned by suffering with depression throughout my life it can be overcome. If you are depressed, I understand this statement seems ludicrous because you can not see the light. However, you can see it if you reach for it. Once again, it does not happen in day. It is a process taking time with the right therapy and recovery group. Nevertheless, it is well worth the fight…just like getting sober.

After years of therapy to help my depression, I was able to get out of bed without a fight. I found there were not enough hours in the day to do everything I wanted to do. Changing my thought process from being continually negative to being positive was a huge factor in helping to lift my depression. (Positive Affirmations discussed in the previous chapter were a great help.) When I started thinking more positive, then all areas of my life started to change. Eventually, I was truly happy for the first time I could remember.

Section III

Truths and Facts: Alcoholism & Drug Addiction

"Twenty years from now you will be more disappointed by the things you didn't do than by the ones you did. So throw off the bowlines. Sail away from the safe harbor. Catch the trade winds in your sails. Explore. Dream. Discover."

– Mark Twain

Chapter 32
The Facts: Educate Yourself on Alcoholism

There are people who still believe that alcoholism and drug addiction is a social problem. The stereotyped image of an alcoholic or addict is they are criminals who have weak morals, poor character and no willpower. Many think alcoholics and addicts should be able to stop drinking and using on their own if they desire. These stereotypes are myths some in our society unfortunately tend to believe as truth.

According to the National Institute on Alcohol Abuse and Alcoholism, "*1 out of every 13 people in the United States has an alcohol problem.*" Even though this is accurate and nearly every American knows an alcoholic, sadly the majority of Americans are not educated on alcoholism. This is disheartening because if more individuals understood the facts about alcohol abuse then I believe more alcoholics and families of alcoholics would seek help. Without being educated on the topic, people are missing out on having happy and productive lives.

This chapter is an extremely important part of the book to me and I strive to fulfill my objective of educating our society about alcoholism. There is much more free information including audio, videos and articles at www.lovedbacktolife.com to answer other questions that you have.

What is alcoholism?

Alcoholism, also known as "alcohol dependence," is a *disease* that includes alcohol craving and continued drinking despite repeated alcohol-related problems, such as losing a job, family, home or getting into trouble with the law. According to the Greater Dallas Council on Alcohol and Drug Abuse it includes four symptoms:

1. Craving – A strong need, or compulsion, to drink.
2. Impaired Control – The inability to limit one's drinking on any given occasion.
3. Physical Dependence – Withdrawal symptoms, such as nausea, sweating, shakiness, or anxiety when alcohol use is stopped after a period of heavy drinking.
4. Tolerance – The need for increasing amounts of alcohol in order to feel its effects.

Is alcoholism a disease? What about drug addiction?

Yes. Alcoholism is classified as a disease by the American Medical Association. The disease is chronic (meaning it lasts a life time), progressive, considered terminal, and has distinguishing symptoms such as excessive, continual loss of control with drinking and the possibility of relapses after periods of abstinence. Despite the negative results an alcoholic will have an uncontrollable craving to drink just like the need for food or water. Alcoholism is determined by a person's genetics, environment, and lifestyle.

Recent scientific research provides overwhelming evidence that not only do drugs interfere with normal brain functioning and create powerful feelings of pleasure, but they also have long-term effects on brain metabolism and activity. At some point, changes occurring in the brain can turn drug abuse into an addiction - a chronic, relapsing illness. Those addicted to drugs suffer from a compulsive drug craving and usage and cannot quit by themselves.

Even though there is not a cure for alcoholism and drug addiction, it is completely treatable. A safe, reputable treatment facility and a recovery support group will help alcoholics and addicts end their obsessive compulsive behaviors.

What is denial?

One of the most disturbing and confusing aspects of addiction is the denial associated with it. The user rejects the notion that his or her use is out of control or it is causing any problems at home or on the job. No matter how badly a user's life is being affected, they refuse to believe alcohol and/or drugs are the cause.

Another problem with denial is it comes and goes. One day an alcoholic realizes they have a problem and wants help and then the next day they emphatically claim they are not alcoholics. This is why it is important to get treatment and find a support group so the chance of denial being present is lessened.

Denial is one of the main reasons why alcoholism is so frustrating. It is difficult for not only alcoholics and drug addicts to handle, but also their families, friends and co-workers. It is extremely exasperating and unnerving to watch someone who has an addiction, is slowing committing suicide and are in complete denial refuse any help.

Who are alcoholics and drug addicts?

Alcoholism and drug addictions have no prejudices. They do not discriminate against any race, gender, religion or socio-economic background. Alcoholics and drug addicts are from every walk of life and include high-powered politicians, lawyers, or doctors, and homeless people living on the streets. Of course, most fall somewhere in between. There are no hard set rules for who can or does become an alcoholic.

What is enabling?

The best description that I have found explaining enabling is outlined by the U.S. Department of Labor as: Any action by another person or an institution that intentionally or unintentionally has the effect of facilitating the continuation of an individual's addictive process. Examples of enabling behavior include:

1. Covering up – Providing alibis, making excuses, or doing an impaired coworker's work rather than allowing it to be known that he or she is not meeting his or her responsibilities.

2. Rationalizing – Developing reasons why the person's continued use is understandable or acceptable.

3. Withdrawing – Avoiding contact with the person who has the problem.

4. Blaming – Getting angry at the individual for not trying hard enough to control his or her use.

5. Controlling – Trying to take responsibility for the person's use by throwing out his or her drugs or cutting off the supply.

6. Threatening – Saying that you will take action (for example, turning the person in) if he or she does not control his or her use, but not following through when he or she continues to use.

Is alcoholism inherited?

The National Institute on Alcohol Abuse and Alcoholism reports research now indicating that alcoholism does run in families. Genetics factors have been found to explain this pattern. A person's environment, such as the influence of friends, stress levels, and the ease of obtaining alcohol, also may influence drinking and the development of alcoholism. Still other factors, such as social support, may help to protect even high-risk people from alcohol problems.

The Institute also reminds us that risk, however, is not destiny. A child of an alcoholic parent will not automatically develop alcoholism. A person with no family history of alcoholism can become alcohol dependent.

Does alcohol affect women differently than men?

Absolutely, says the National Institute on Alcohol Abuse and Alcoholism. Women become more impaired than men after drinking the same amount of alcohol, even when differences in body weight are taken into account. This is because women's bodies have less water than men's bodies. Because alcohol mixes with body water, a given amount of alcohol becomes more highly concentrated in a woman's body than in a man's.

The Institute also states chronic alcohol abuse takes a heavier physical toll on women than on men. Alcohol dependence and related medical problems, such as brain, heart and liver damage, progress more rapidly in women than in men.

What are the effects of alcoholism?

As stated earlier, alcoholism is a disease and can be fatal and is incurable. With alcoholism there are many different kinds of effects and they can appear in a variety of forms. An alcoholic can drive drunk and get into an accident, get arrested for Driving While Intoxicated (DWI), go to jail, destroy all relationships, sacrifice all material possessions and lose all self-respect.

The best and easiest way to understand the source for this topic is the NA and AA recovery zone website. (If you go to www.lovedbacktolife.com, you will find a link). The Recovery zone explains there are two types of effects from alcoholism. *The first is mental and the second is physical.* The first is an insane mental obsession and the need to get more alcohol under any circumstances. This need drives people to do senseless deeds.

This obsession changes the person emotionally into someone you would not recognize. The alcoholic when drinking demonstrates inappropriate actions they would never do when they are sober.

The second type of effect of alcoholism is physical. Alcoholics can suffer from liver disease and brain damage. Since alcohol is a toxin, the body of the alcoholic responds to such. Our body's natural detoxification system (endocrine system) treats alcohol like a poison. As a result, since the liver plays a major role in the endocrine system it is largely affected by alcohol. Alcohol will slowly kill the liver until it becomes diseased or fails.

Alcohol also attacks the brain. It kills large amounts of brain cells with the more a person consumes. This causes short-term memory loss and eventually will lead to what people call "wet brain." This is when the alcoholics mind no longer functions normally and they are in a pre-vegetable state. The person can not speak properly and usually will lose control of their bladder and bowel functions. So essentially an alcoholic can drink themselves to a point where they can no longer speak, can barely move, and has to wear diapers so they do not urinate or defecate on themselves.

The American Council for Drug Education states repeated alcohol abuse can cause cardiological problems including elevated blood pressure, increased heart rate, risk of stroke, and heart failure. The respiratory system is also in danger from alcohol intake. Dangers include respiratory depression and failure, pneumonia, tuberculosis, and lung abscesses. Additionally, alcohol abuse increases the risk of mouth and throat cancer.

What is "binge" drinking?

When I binge drank, I would drink heavily over a several day period. Sometimes it would be a weekend or a vacation. Occasionally, I would miss work for a day or two and continue drinking. However, the most widely used definition for binge drinking today is a man consuming 5 or more drinks in a row and a woman consuming four or more drinks in a row at least once in a two week period. Very heavy binge drinking would be considered having three drinking sprees within two weeks.

Binge drinkers often have a difficult time admitting they are alcoholics or have drinking problems because they rationalize that they do not drink every day. However, heavy consumption of alcohol in short periods can also mean a person may be an alcoholic and drinking alcohol heavily can also cause physical damage to both the body and the brain.

What does it mean to "hit bottom"?

When you hear an alcoholic or a drug addict refer to hitting bottom, it typically means the last demoralizing incident happening to them and opening their eyes. It made them seek out help. In other words, it is the place an alcoholic/addict arrives where they absolutely know they have a problem and do not want to live the way they are living anymore.

Every person's bottom is different and there is no set rule for when a person will hit bottom and desire help. Some alcoholics and drug addicts' eyes open when they get a DWI or DUI and have to go to jail. For others it may take a divorce, loss of child custody, car wrecks, bankruptcy, physical ailments, emotional duress, or homelessness. Hopefully, since alcoholism is a progressive disease and continues getting worse over time, an alcoholic will get desperate enough and hit bottom early on in his drinking career. Hitting bottoms is an undeterminable destiny for alcoholics and addicts…you never know if or when the time will come.

What is an intervention?

If a family member, friend or co-worker has an alcohol or drug addiction, keep in mind they can not get sober and/or clean on their own. They will need assistance getting the aid needed to begin the recovery process. This is where an intervention process is important in helping your loved one find help. An intervention is where family, friends, and co-workers confront the addicted person in a group. Usually the objective of an intervention is to have the alcoholic/addict go immediately into a treatment facility. I have repeatedly heard of interventions going array because the families do not understand how to handle and conduct an intervention properly. In many situations getting a professional who is an intervention specialist is essential to help carefully plan and perform the intervention.

Sometimes the intervention is successful and the alcoholic/addict may agree to go to treatment. Other times the addict becomes violent, belligerent, and hostile. You can not predict their behavior so be prepared for any kind of reaction.

If you are serious about understanding an intervention more in-depth then I highly recommend a book called *Love First* by Jeff Jay and Debra Jay. The book goes into great detail about interventions. The author himself is a recovering alcoholic and he describes the intervention process that saved his life. His first hand-experience explains how to have a successful intervention by taking the proper course of action.

Does alcohol and drug treatment really work?

It definitely works, yes. Addiction is often described as a chronic relapsing condition characterized by waves of abuse, decreased use, and then more abuse.

For many alcoholics and drug addicts, more than one treatment episode may be required before improvements (reductions in use or sustained remission) are seen. According to the Greater Dallas Council on Alcohol and Drug Abuse, studies show that after six months, treatment for alcoholism is successful for 40–70% of the patients. The improvement rate for people completing substance abuse treatment is comparable to that of people treated for asthma and other chronic, relapsing health conditions.

If a person is unable to go to an inpatient treatment facility they can easily find an Alcoholics Anonymous or Narcotics Anonymous meeting where they live by looking in the phone book or on the Internet.

What exactly is "detox"?

The most straightforward and uncomplicated explanation of "detox" was posted by the Greater Dallas Council on Alcohol and Drug Abuse. It states, drinking alcohol or using a drug over time eventually causes a physical dependence. The actual stopping of drinking alcohol or using drugs results in what is known as withdrawal. Detox, short for detoxification (withdrawal), with medical supervision and assistance is potentially very dangerous and should not be attempted. Alcohol and or other drug detox can result in severe consequences—such as the delirium tremors (aka the "DTs"), seizures, convulsions, shakes, nausea, hallucinations, high blood pressure, anxiety, headaches, and insomnia.

The Council also describes the term detox as referring to the detoxifying of the residual toxins left in the human body as a result of taking alcohol and other drugs. From a medical prospective, detox is the process of medically managing the body's physical withdrawal from alcohol and other drugs to minimize the possible side effects and help prevent potentially harmful consequences. There are a variety of methods for the actual medical process of detox.

The length of time required for detox depends on the process being utilized. In general, alcohol detox, when done in a medical environment, can take anywhere from 3–5 days. For drugs such as heroin, opiates, methadone, or benzodiazepines the time can range from 5–7 days for a medically supervised detox.The medical process of detox usually includes administering a variety of substances to relieve the withdrawal symptoms and minimize the potentially harmful consequences. The Greater Dallas Council on Alcohol and Drug Abuse stresses the fact that since there could be harmful effects of detoxing it is highly suggested to have medical supervision when doing so.

Does alcoholism affect older people differently?

Absolutely. The effects of drinking alcohol vary with age. The following are results of how alcohol reacts in older persons:

1. Reactions are slower.
2. Unable to hear as usual.
3. Unable to see as usual.
4. Lower tolerance to the effects of alcohol.

Since older persons have an even lower tolerance rate compared to younger drinkers, they have a higher risk of having car accidents, injuries and more immediate negative affects on their bodies.

Also, those in their golden years tend to be taking more medication than the younger generations.There are numerous drugs that are harmful when combined with alcohol and many of these drugs are taken by senior citizens.This is another very important factor for older persons not to consume alcohol. It is also damaging physically if a person drinks who has ulcers, high blood pressure and liver problems.

Are there medications to help treat alcoholism?

Yes. According to the National Institute on Alcohol Abuse and Alcoholism, there are two types of medications that can help a person who has alcoholism.There are medications such as tranquilizers called benzodiazepines (i.e. Valium, Librium) available to help when detoxing. However, these drugs are only used the first few days of treatment and any medications taken need to be prescribed by a doctor and used only as directed.

The second type of medication sometimes given to alcoholics that may help them remain sober is called naltrexone (ReVia). When combined with counseling, this medication can lessen the craving for alcohol. Another older, but similar medication is disulfiram (Antabuse); this deters the alcoholic from drinking because it causes nausea, vomiting and other unpleasant reactions when combined with alcohol.

Why can't alcoholics quit on their own?

Most people who have alcohol problems believe they can stop drinking on their own without any help. This may result in short periods of abstinence, but most eventually begin drinking and using again and do not acquire long-term sobriety. Once alcoholics become obsessed with drinking, it takes over their entire body mentally and physically. The obsession cultivates, increases, intensifies and explodes into an irrational craving for alcohol. The consequences of the alcoholics' drinking matters little or nothing to them. This obsession baffles not only the alcoholic but those around him as well. The alcoholic with this obsession becomes unstoppable without the proper treatment and support group.

What is a 12-Step Recovery Program?

The 12 Step Recovery Programs are used nearly everywhere when coping with alcoholism and drug addiction. It is probably the most regularly used program of recovery. The program consists of 12 Steps to which the alcoholic and drug addict are introduced. They are then taught how each step works and how to move on to the next. These programs encourage sponsorship and companionship among those in the group. The first 12 Step program was introduced in the 1930s as Alcoholics Anonymous. Since then, the 12 Steps have extended into many other groups including Narcotics Anonymous, Alan-on (for families of the alcoholic and addict), Overeaters Anonymous, Adult Children of Alcoholics, Gamblers Anonymous, Smokers Anonymous, Cocaine Anonymous and numerous other organizations. You can find more specific information on line at www.lovedbacktolife.com.

Alcoholics Anonymous alone has millions of members in the United States and the 12 Step way of recovery has proven it is effective and successful for many.

Chapter 33
Treatment and Recovery Groups...Do they really work?

Absolutely, yes! I personally would not be sober today if it was not for treatment and my support groups. It has been proven over and over again that alcoholism and drug addiction can be overcome with the right treatment. I highly recommend a treatment center that will introduce an alcoholic and/or addict to the 12 Step Program. Most treatment centers will have several professional psychiatrists on staff and the patient will also be introduced to Alcoholics Anonymous and Narcotic Anonymous meetings. These meetings are where the 12 Steps of Recovery are discussed in detail. A person attempting sobriety can observe first hand how it is possible to quit using and drinking. This is where they are exposed to other alcoholics and addicts who have been alcohol and drug free for many years.

Long-term abstinence and recovery can occur if a person is dedicated to their recovery. Most alcoholics and addicts who have multiple years of recovery are still involved with their support groups. Those alcoholics and addicts who lose touch with their support groups often have their denial kick back in gear at some point. They begin to believe they are no longer alcoholics or addicts and they can occasionally drink or use drugs "socially." This begins their downward spiral to bottoming out with their addiction again. Sadly, many of these people do not get sober and clean again. An alcoholic and drug addict never knows if that next drink or drug they pick up could lead to their demise.

Sometimes more than one treatment process might be necessary for the alcoholic and/or addict to find recovery. It is common for people to relapse several times before achieving long-term sobriety. It is important to keep in mind a relapse does not mean a person can not ever find recovery. Everyone needs to remember it is a temporary set back and the alcoholic and/or addict must immediately seek help again either professionally or in their support group - preferably both. Even people with long term recovery sometimes relapse. Alcoholism is a sly and shrewd disease creeping up on an alcoholic without having any preconceived notions of drinking. There are no guarantees.

Treatment and recovery for alcoholics and addicts can significantly improve their quality of life. They feel better physically and emotionally and they perform better at work and at home. According to the National Council on Alcoholism and Drug Dependence, "Research shows conclusively that successful prevention and treatment leads to reductions in traffic fatalities, crime, unwanted pregnancy, child abuse, HIV, cancer and heart disease."

The Council also notes that employers will be happy to learn that once an alcoholic and/or addict receives treatment for their addiction the following happened:

- Absenteeism decreased by 89%
- Tardiness decreased by 92%
- Problems with supervisors decreased by 56%
- Mistakes in work decreased by 70%
- Incomplete work decreased by 81%

There are millions and millions of alcoholics and drug addicts who recover from their addictions. These addictions are treatable. Alcoholics and/or addicts in recovery who remain abstinent from their addictions lead very productive and inspiring lives.

Chapter 34
What Happens at Support Group Meetings?

One of the most daunting experiences is going to a meeting for the first time. Walking through the door is a courageous, but terrifying, step for an alcoholic. A person never knows what to expect and they usually have a preconceived picture of the meeting in a dingy room filled densely with cigarette smoke and ungroomed people who are shaking and drinking massive amounts of coffee. This is not the typical Alcoholics Anonymous or Narcotics Anonymous meetings today. Many of the meetings and groups are non-smoking or have specific smoking sections with fans designed to rid the room of smoke. Usually people are not detoxing or shaking during the meetings. The majority of the people at these meetings are already in recovery so they are well-groomed and appropriately attired. The stereotypical meeting does often include massive amounts of coffee being consumed, but do not fear if you do not drink coffee…it is not a requirement. My suggestion when first going to a meeting or a new group is not to over think the situation…just take the plunge. Do not hesitate. Walk right through the doors, introduce yourself to other alcoholics and/or addicts, find a seat, sit back and listen to the meeting.

There are many different types of support group meetings. Most support groups focus on the 12 Steps of Recovery. Alcoholics and Drug Addicts go to Alcoholics Anonymous meetings and/or Narcotics Anonymous meetings to find recovery. Alanon also uses the 12 Step Program for families affected by alcoholism and drug addiction along with Alateen for teenagers.

Alcoholics Anonymous was the original 12 Step Program and today numerous other organizations have used the same steps with minor adjustments for the basis of overcoming many other addictions. These programs include: Narcotics Anonymous, Alanon, Alateen, Overeaters Anonymous, Gamblers Anonymous, Sex & Love Addiction Anonymous, Adult Children of Alcoholics Anonymous, Nicotine Anonymous, Cocaine Anonymous, Chemically Dependent Anonymous, Co-dependents Anonymous, and many more. All of these meetings can be found in the phone book or on the Internet.

These support groups are non-profit organizations that have no fees or dues. A basket is passed around the room, and if those attending have a dollar or two to donate, then they do so.

The people at these meetings all have the same addiction, disease or problem they are trying to understand, cope with and recover from. The group comes together to listen, talk and help each other to recover from their addiction. It provides emotional and spiritual support for those who desire recovery.

There is a vast array of people at recovery meetings. Alcoholics and drug addicts range from being a wealthy doctor who has nearly lost his license to an alcoholic who has not been able to work in many years. It does not matter what you do or who you are at these meetings. Everyone there suffers from the same disease of addiction. They are all there for the same reason…to stay alcohol and drug free.

The meeting schedules differ from group to group so it is important to contact the group or find the schedules on the Internet. In a large metropolitan city, you can find a meeting nearly 24 hours a day. There are meetings starting at 6:00 am and there are some that begin at midnight. Generally, meetings are an hour long.

There are discussion meetings and speaker meetings. Discussion meetings usually cover a specific topic and speaker meetings involve a person in recovery talking about their experience, strength and hope. It is suggested a new person go to both discussion and speaker meetings.

Recovery depends on a combination of factors. However, it is of utmost importance a new person in the program finds a temporary sponsor. A sponsor assists a person with the 12 Steps and offers advice and guidance. Without a sponsor a person can become lost and not find true recovery because they are not being guided through the program. By practicing the principals of the Steps and doing the work associated with each step, a person can find true happiness and success in sobriety. Seldom does a person who does not get a sponsor and work the steps achieve long-term sobriety.

Nowadays, Alcoholics Anonymous and Narcotics Anonymous have more groups, meetings and people in recovery than ever before. No matter where you are traveling or living, there is a meeting somewhere close. An alcoholic and/or addict can not use the lame excuse they can't find a meeting. They are nearly everywhere all throughout the day and night. If a person desires recovery then it is available to them.

Chapter 35
Some People "Just Don't Get It..." Etiquette 101 for Socializing with a Sober Alcoholic

The following are questions that the recovering alcoholic and drug addict are often asked by people who *"Just Don't Get It…"* The suggested answers are responses recommended for recovering alcoholics and addicts. I am frequently surprised how little people know about alcoholism and drug addiction when millions and millions of people in this country are alcoholics and drug addicts. My desire is once you have read this book and this chapter you understand and know the *"etiquette"* when dealing with a person who is in recovery. I sincerely hope you become one of the people who *"Get It…."*

Question: I know you've been in recovery for along time, so… you can drink now, right?
Suggested Answer: I can't drink if I don't want to break out in spots…. Texas, New York, Colorado. You never know where I'll end up if I take a drink. (Then laugh because they'll think you are kidding.)

*****

Question: I know you're in recovery, but can't you just drink one drink?
Suggested Answer: I've never had just one drink of alcohol in my life. Do you really think if I could drink just one drink that I would end up being the alcoholic in recovery that I am? (Then laugh because sometimes other people's ignorance is funny.)

*****

Question: I know you are in recovery, but can't you just drink beer and wine?
Suggested Answer: I can drink whatever I choose. I choose not to drink beer and wine because the side of the can says it has alcohol in it. Besides, I've had enough alcohol to last me a lifetime. (Then smile because

if they only knew how much you actually did drink they'd never have asked the question.)

*****

Question: I know you really don't drink and are in recovery, but let me get you one drink that's really watered down, okay?
Suggested Answer: Sure, just as long as you are ready to take care of my wife/husband, kids, and bills when I disappear on a drinking binge for a couple of months? (Then smile as they look perplexed.)

*****

Question: I know you are in recovery, so how much are you allowed to drink now?
Suggested Answer: I don't know, how many do you think I can drink and still be sober? (Then smile and look like you are anxiously waiting for their answer.)

*****

Question: I don't believe that alcoholism is really a disease, do you?
Suggested Answer: I'm not a doctor but according to the American Medical Association alcoholism is a disease. Be careful, you might catch it! (Then laugh while poking them with your finger.)

*****

Question: Since you are not drinking and can drive, will you go to the liquor store and buy us some more?
Suggested Answer: None. Just stare at them blankly. (Don't laugh.)

*****

Question: I know you don't drink anymore, but you still do drugs… don't you?
Suggested Answer: Well, alcohol is a drug, but sure, why not…rehab sounds great again! Are you paying for it this time? (Then laugh.)

*****

Question: You've been sober awhile now, why do you still go to those meetings?
Suggested Answer: Because I am completely insane and I do the same thing over and over again and expect different results. So if I don't keep going back, I forget that I'm an alcoholic and then I'd end up drinking and completely messing up my life by losing everything, going to jail and best yet, there is a high possibility that I would die.

OR

Suggested Answer: It's a secret. (Then smile mysteriously.)
(I realize the first answer is the honest one, but the person will probably not understand any of what you just said and only think you are crazy. So, let's stick with the latter answer.)

*****

Question: How do you have fun without alcohol?
Suggested Answer: I have much more fun without alcohol, and I remember everything I do the next day I don't puke; I don't get arrested; and I remember where I parked my car. (Then smile understandingly.)

(HINT: If a person is asking this question, they obviously can't have fun without drinking and probably have a problem with alcohol. Be grateful that you are in recovery and save them a seat at the support group. Hopefully, they will find their way in.)

Chapter 36
Take the Test: Are You an Alcoholic? Are You a Drug Addict?

The following is a test to help determine if you may be an alcoholic. This test has been compiled after much research. It was created by sober alcoholics and addicts and the questions have been chosen because they could identify with them from their own personal experiences and knowledge. You do not have to identify with every question. If you have a problem with drugs, these tests can be used to determine if you may be an addict also. Just replace the word alcohol with drug and answer the questions. Since alcohol is a drug, I believe it is important to abstain from alcohol as well as drugs when dealing with addiction. The objective of this test is to aid you in determining if help and/or treatment are needed in your situation. Be truthful when answering these questions. It is suggested that you answer the questions in private so you feel comfortable answering them honestly. My hope is you will find the needed answers and become closer to finding the necessary direction for a peaceful and blissful life.

SELF TEST FOR ALCOHOLISM

1. Do you feel guilty when you drink?
2. When you wake up in the morning, do you forget what you did the night before?
3. Have you missed days of work because of your drinking?
4. Is your drinking contributing to financial problems?
5. Do you use alcohol to escape difficulties you are having in your life?
6. Do you get upset, irritated or angry when people talk about your drinking?
7. Do you drink when you are alone?
8. Do you drink when you are at work?
9. Have you ever stayed drunk for days at a time?
10. Have you ever moved or changed jobs to avoid the consequences of your drinking?

11. Have you ever made promises about cutting down or stopping drinking and not been able to keep them?
12. Is drinking making it difficult to deal with your family?
13. Are you relieved when your family is not around so that you can drink?
14. Do you find yourself drinking at inferior places and with people you usually would not associate with when you are not drinking?
15. Does drinking come before your family responsibilities?
16. Do you drink in the morning?
17. Do you sometimes feel remorse over things you did or said when you were drinking?
18. Have you tried to minimize your drinking by switching alcoholic beverages or brands?
19. Have you ever had the morning shakes and need to have a drink to calm them?
20. Do you take satisfaction in knowing that you drink more than your friends can?
21. Do you get angry with yourself when you binge drink?
22. Do you feel that you can do much more with your life if you were not drinking?
23. Does your family and/or friends make excuses for you often because of your drinking?
24. Do you have difficulties doing the same tasks that use to be easy for you?
25. Are you not motivated to accomplish goals the way you used to be?
26. Do you find your family, friends and co-workers are doing more tasks for you because you are unable?
27. Have you been seen by a doctor for your drinking?
28. Have you ever been arrested because of drinking?
29. Do you sometimes feel life is not worth living?
30. Is there any kind of negative backlash in your life because of your drinking?

If you answered "*YES*" to any one or two of the above questions then you could have a problem with drinking. If you answered "*YES*" to three or more of the questions then it is probable that you have a serious drinking problem and may be an alcoholic. Please talk to a professional or find a support group in your area like Alcoholics Anonymous or Narcotics Anonymous. You can find more contact information about these groups by going to www.lovedbacktolife.com or you can find meetings in your area by looking in the phone book or on the Internet.

Chapter 37
Take the Test: Are You Co-Dependent? Do you have an Alcoholic or Addict in your life?

<u>Co-Dependent Definition:</u> of or pertaining to a relationship in which one person is physically or psychologically addicted, as to alcohol, drugs or gambling etc., and the other person is psychologically dependent on the first in an unhealthy way.

The following self-test will help you determine how an alcoholic in your life is affecting your behaviors and actions. There has been much research to compile this test and it has been created by recovering co-dependents. It is important to remember that alcoholism and addiction is considered a "Family Disease" because everyone close to an alcoholic and/or addict is influenced negatively. Families and friends of alcoholics and/or addicts can be just as mentally ill as the alcoholic and/or addict because of all the turmoil that they have experienced over the years dealing with the alcoholic and/or addict. The objective of this test is to aid you in determining if help is needed in your situation. If you have an addict in your life, just replace the words "problem drinker" with "addict." Be truthful when answering these questions. It is suggested that you answer the questions in private so you feel comfortable answering them honestly. My hope is you will find the needed answers and become closer to finding the necessary direction for a happy, healthy and serene life.

SELF TEST FOR CODEPENDENCY

1. Do you wait up and not sleep until the problem drinker gets home?
2. Do you feel embarrassed around your friends and other family members because of the problem drinker's behavior?
3. Do you make excuses and cover up when the problem drinker makes mistakes or does something inappropriate?

4. Do you lie about how much the problem drinker actually drinks?
5. Do you feel like you can not live without the problem drinker in your life?
6. Has the problem drinker broken promises to you about quitting drinking?
7. Do you threaten the problem drinker and then not follow through with your threat?
8. Do you let the problem drinker control how you feel?
9. Do you constantly worry about the problem drinker and what will happen next?
10. Do you believe everything would change if the problem drinker quit drinking?
11. Do you feel responsible for the problem drinkers drinking and actions?
12. Do you think you can "fix" the problem?
13. Are you physically getting sick such as nausea, upset stomach, eating less, and/or headaches because of the problem drinker's actions?
14. Do you take to heart the negative things that the problem drinker sometimes says about you?
15. Do you often feel alone, sad, anxious, angry, and/or resentful?
16. Do you often not like yourself and how your life has turned out?
17. Are you doing tasks that the problem drinker used to do?
18. Is the situation affecting your work?
19. Have you stopped socializing with friends and family because of the problem drinker?
20. Do you feel there is no hope in your life?
21. Do you feel the problem drinker will never change?
22. Do you sometimes feel superior to the problem drinker and often put them down?
23. Do your moods change quickly because of the problem drinker's behaviors and actions?
24. If there are children in the house, are their personalities changing because of emotional stress? (For example: low grades in school, dropping out of extra-curricular activities, changing friends, withdrawing, changing the way they dress, etc.)

25. *However this may apply:* Do you use sex as a weapon to manipulate the problem drinker (give them sex or not give them sex) as a reward or punishment?

If you answered *"YES"* to any of these questions then you are allowing the problem drinker, alcoholic or drug addict's actions affect your life and are considered to be co-dependent. If you answered *"YES"* to three or more of these questions then you have become part of the downward progression of alcoholism and/or drug addiction. Please talk to a professional or find a support group in your area like Alanon. Alanon is a support group for families of alcoholics and addicts. You can find more contact information about different Alanon groups by going to www.lovedbacktolife.com or you can find meetings in your area by looking in the phone book or on the Internet.

Chapter 38
For Parents!
Take the Test:
What is Your Assessment for Addiction?

This test has been included because it is essential that parents comprehend how their actions using alcohol and drugs affect their children dramatically. The questions in this test have been researched and parents who are in recovery have helped create the questions. Children are a reflection of their environment and their behaviors are a direct result of what they experience at home. The parents' habits with alcohol and drugs are creating the norm for their children. Young children and teenagers will copy what they see first-hand. Not only will they develop the same habits, but their self-esteem and self-confidence are affected by what surrounds them. The negativity alcohol and drugs bring into the home affects a child for the rest of their lives.

The objective of this test is to aid you in determining if help is needed in your situation. Be truthful when answering these questions. It is suggested you answer the questions in private so you feel comfortable answering them honestly. My hope is you will find the needed answers and become closer to finding the necessary help and/or taking positive actions for you and your children.

Parents: What is your assessment for drinking and using drugs?

1. Have your children ever seen you drunk from alcohol or high when using drugs?
2. Have you ever missed your child's special events because you were drinking or using drugs?
3. Do you take your child with you to the liquor store when you are buying alcohol?
4. Do you let your child pour your alcoholic beverages?
5. Do you take sleeping pills (over the counter or prescribed) to fall asleep at night?
6. Do you smoke cigarettes?
7. Have you ever warned your child about the dangers of smoking while you are smoking? Answer this question again, but

replace smoking with drinking and then replace it with drugs.

8. Have you ever been drunk or high when driving your children in a car?
9. Do you sometimes "pass out" at home when you are drinking or using drugs?
10. Have your children heard you arguing with your spouse about the amount of alcohol they drink or drugs they use?
11. Do you often drink alcohol at special family occasions around the children?
12. Have your children ever asked you to stop drinking, smoking or using drugs?
13. When you are upset, do you automatically take a drink or a drug to "calm your nerves"?
14. Do you smoke marijuana?
15. Do your children know you smoke marijuana? Do they know it is illegal and harmful to your health?
16. When you are feeling down or depressed, do you use alcohol or drugs as a "pick-me-up"?
17. When you entertain at home, do you automatically ask your friends if they want an alcoholic beverage?
18. Have you yelled and said things you should not have said to your children when drinking or using drugs?
19. Have you ever let your young children taste an alcoholic beverage?
20. Is alcohol always present and kept in your home?
21. Do you or your spouse sometimes yell at each other and say things to hurt each other and the children can hear?
22. Do you ever get shaky and jumpy when drinking coffee?
23. Do you have to drink a coffee in the morning to "wake up"?
24. Do you sometimes take diet pills to lose weight?
25. In regards to alcohol and drugs, do you not conduct yourself in the same way you want your children to act?

If you answered *"YES"* to any of the questions then you need to assess your role as a parent very carefully. It is imperative that you realize that what your children see you doing is what they will also do. Addiction of any sort is a vicious family cycle passed down from generation to generation. Until someone steps out of the cycle and seeks help, it will continue to progress. If you decide that you need help in a certain area, find professional help. There are many support groups such as Alcoholics Anonymous, Narcotics Anonymous and Nicotine Anonymous available. You can find more contact information about these groups by going to www.lovedbacktolife.com or you can find meetings in your area by looking in the phone book or on the Internet.

Section IV

Sober Success Stories

*"Although the world is full of suffering,
it is also full of the overcoming of it."*

– Helen Keller

The Sober Success Stories

There are *"18 million alcoholics in America" (National Council on Alcoholism and Drug Dependence)* or *"1 out of every 13 people have a drinking problem" (National Institute on Alcoholism and Alcohol Abuse)*...millions are sober alcoholics who are breaking the stigma of alcoholism and leading extraordinary lives.

Many sober alcoholics have survived inconceivable circumstances and are now thriving. However, the stigma of being a "drunk" is always attached. The following inspiring stories of sober alcoholics and their journeys will not only help you recognize what incredibly fascinating people they are, but hopefully you will also gain respect for sober alcoholics as a whole.

These people are miracles and have followed similar paths to sobriety with different experiences. I am anticipating that after reading these remarkably successful journeys many will re-evaluate the stigma often attached to being an alcoholic even after many years of sobriety.

The stories also suggest that anyone who has a drinking or drug problem has options available to positively change their lives get clean and stay sober.

We would love to hear "Sober Success Stories." Please go to www.lovedbacktolife.com for more information or you can email us at stories@amycrowell.net

Chapter 39
Alcoholic Fog & Blackouts
By: Tony Z.

"Out of an estimated 5.3 million convicted offenders under the supervision of criminal justice authorities found that nearly 40% of these offenders, about 2 million, had been using alcohol at the time of the offense for which they were convicted." [97]

My story begins in New York City about 50 years ago. I do not remember my early years very much, but I do know we traveled a lot. My most vivid memory is when I was 7 years-old and my dad unexpectedly came home from work and told my mother he was leaving. It would be seven and a half years later before I saw him again.

My mother moved us from Indianapolis to New York City where her family lived and we lived on welfare and second-hand clothes. I was the second of five kids and my older brother felt that he was the man of the house. In order to keep the other kids in line, I became the example of what would happen if they did not do as they were told. This meant I endured a lot of beatings, teasing and anything else that came to his mind. I escaped by hiding at first, and later I began sniffing glue and paint thinner. However, I did not like the way it felt so I did not do it often. By the time my dad returned my brother had joined the army and my sister who was a year younger than I was, had gotten very ill and died.

We moved to Maine where I had high hopes things would be different and they were, but not the way I was hoping. I felt even more like an outsider, and I had very few friends. Then one day I met a few guys at the bus stop who asked me if I wanted to get "high" and I said sure. I began smoking pot and taking acid before school, and I was having beer parties on the weekend. This went on from the time I was 15 years-old until a couple of years later when I quit school and tried to hitch hike to California. My plans failed and I ended up joining the Navy instead.

I figured once I had joined the Navy I was a real man and could do whatever I wanted. Later, I would learn the Navy did not agree with me. Instead of beer, I started drinking whiskey because I found I did not need to drink as much whiskey to get to the place where I did not care or remember. I would drink everyday if we were in port, yet when we went to sea I had no problem being without it for months at a time. This helped me to believe I did not have a problem with drinking.

The Navy saw my drinking in a different way and they did not feel someone who was only 18 years-old should be drinking as much as I was. They sent me to my first AA meeting. I went in looked around and felt that it was not for me. A few months later the Navy and I departed company, which at the time I felt was the best thing. Now I could drink and collect unemployment checks for awhile. My warped thinking told me that I had made it… I could drink every day and collect checks. What more could I want?

It was not long before the money ran out and I needed to get a real job. However, instead I decided to hitch hike to California again. By now I was drinking everyday and moving across the country was one way to keep people from knowing where I was and what I was doing. Due to the amount of alcohol I was consuming and the way I was living, I lost track of time. At some point, I hooked up with a guy who drove a moving truck and hired me as his full-time helper. He lived in south Dallas and when he was home I would sleep in the back of the trailer at night. For a short time my drinking slowed down. But that did not last long. We were heading out west when we had a wreck. As a result, there was no work and I did not have a place to live.

Once again, my drinking became a full-time occupation and at some point in 1976 I woke up in the Dallas County jail. I was being charged with a number of different felonies. Let's just say that things were not looking very good for me. It did not help the situation that I was considered a vagrant with no address, no family in Texas and no means of support. There was talk that I would be getting 25 years to life in prison. After sitting in jail for 6 months, all I had to do was plead guilty to one charge and my time would be set for five years. I jumped at this chance and everything was arranged.

There is no need to go into detail about what jail is like. Let's just say it's an experience that was terrible, putting it mildly. The bottom line is that after six months in the county jail and an additional two years, four months and eleven days in prison, I got paroled to New York City. My aunt and uncle lived in New York City so I went there because I was told that I could not go back to my folks' home.

When I got out of prison in Huntsville I was told there were three things I needed to do. First, do not stay in Huntsville. Second, do not mess with any women in Huntsville, and third, do not drink in Huntsville.

I followed most of their directions except before getting on the bus to Dallas where I picked up a pint of whiskey. When I got to Dallas I caught a plane to New York City, and I do not remember any of the flight. I do know at sometime I met with my parole officer who made it clear that as long as I stayed out of trouble things would be okay. He also said if he ever got a call saying I was in jail for anything that he would send me back to Texas to finish my time.

After meeting with my parole officer, I did not drink again while I was on parole. I got a job and was making a living and learning a trade with the help of my uncle. I was able to move out of my family's basement and into my own apartment. I was also able to buy myself a used car. Things were going good for me and I believed that I had learned a very valuable lesson. I was becoming a productive member of society.

Then I got off of parole and I was once again free to do whatever I wanted to do. After having a period of time when I did not drink, the last thing I had on my mind was I had a drinking problem. I chalked up my past experiences to being young and stupid. Now that I was older and had a good job, things would be different. So I started drinking again, but not to excess - at first. I would have a couple of beers each night. I told myself that I was not going to drink whiskey again because I knew it made me do crazy things. I did not want to end up sleeping behind bars again.

This lasted for a few weeks or a couple of months - who knows. However, one night I was driving home from work and when I crossed over the bridge instead of bearing left to go home to Brooklyn, I went straight and headed out of town. Once again, I jumped off into the abyss of alcoholism and my memory fails me. I know that I sold my car down south somewhere in order to buy some more booze. Also, the idea of going back to New York never crossed my mind. I did not care what I left behind or if anyone was worried about me being gone. I know I drank a lot for the next few years and I was in an ever-present alcoholic fog of coming in and out of blackouts.

I also know in the beginning of October 1982, I woke up in the Houston City Jail. I did not even want to open my eyes because I knew where I was. Some how the idea of being locked up just made sense to me. This way everyone would know where I was, and I would be able to stop the living nightmare that was my life. When I went in front of the judge, I had no idea what I did or what I was going to be charged with. I was lucky. It turned out to be a Public Intoxication or PI with a fine of $52.50 or 30 days at the pea farm. He also asked me two questions, and it was the first time someone *asked* me instead of *told* me what to do. First, I was asked if I felt like I had a problem with alcohol. Second, I was asked if I wanted to learn a way to get sober and stay sober. I said "yes" to both of the questions. I also told the gentleman that I would go anywhere and do anything provided that he was at the pea farm within two hours of me being released. Because I knew with no money in my pockets it would take me just about that long to find something to drink.

He explained he would get my fine suspended if I agreed to enter a detox center run by the city. I quickly agreed to this before he changed his mind. So I went to my third 12 step meeting and picked up my first desire chip. (A desire chip is a coin that 12 step programs give to those who have the desire to stay sober for a 24 hour period.) I knew I would do this for a few days and disappear once again into what was for me a normal life.

At one of the meetings I was standing outside smoking with a guy, who was a counselor. He had lived a life just like mine and he was now sober for 6½ years. He said that I needed to get my head off the street and my ass into a seat in the meeting. He went on to explain that when drunks like me get sober for a few days or weeks we start thinking about drinking again. We forget what hell our life was up to this point. He told me I could keep doing what I was doing and I would either end up locked in a jail cell, trapped in a nut ward for the rest of my life or dead either from someone killing me or me killing myself. I don't know why, but I stayed and listened to what was being said at the meeting that day.

I started reading the 12 step books, going to meetings and doing the things asked of me. At the time, because of my experiences and everything I had put myself through, I felt like I was a very old for only being 28 years-old. I got my first real job in sobriety flipping burgers and my boss was only 19 years-old. Nevertheless, I kept moving forward and soon I was living in my own apartment again. I also had an old pick up to drive to and from work and to the meetings each night. I found a sponsor to help me with the 12 steps. As the weeks turned into months and the months into years, my life changed.

I got married and we had a baby girl. I went from flipping burgers to fixing tractor trailers and my life was great. However, most of the time I still had feelings of being less than those around me. The recovery steps talked about the Higher Power who everyone was calling "God" and that was not working for me. I could believe He would keep me sober, but I could not believe He would forgive me for the life I had been living.

I may not have remembered all of it, but I was sure it was nothing to be proud of.

I had fallen into the same old trap again. I was comparing how I felt on the inside with how others looked on the outside, and I always came out with the short end of the stick. It had been over five years since I had had a drink. My past life seemed just that – past. However, the day I dreaded came like I had read in the 12 step books and as I had heard in the meetings. I started drinking again. I did not start drinking because my body needed it, but because my mind (or more to the point - the disease in my head) said it was okay. This time, it would be different. It was definitely different. I found I could still work and drink. There were some days when I needed to drink more and work less. I somehow managed to keep my job, but I lost my wife and daughter along the way.

There were car wrecks and motorcycle wrecks I blamed on someone else and were never my own fault. I insisted that these accidents were not because I was drinking. I began a new cycle of living in and out of the doors of the program, only managing to get either a few weeks or months of sobriety before I drank again. Somewhere along the line I got married a 2nd time and moved from Baytown to Dallas. I was hoping my new wife, job and surroundings would help my situation. Well, geographical cures do not work so it is obvious how the story turns out. I ended up losing that wife also.

One day I came to out of a blackout during a newcomer's meeting. I did not know how long I had been there or even what day of the week it was. All I knew for sure was I could not go down this path anymore. Whatever fight there was left in me was gone, and I was a broken man.

Once again I started down the road would lead me to a sober, happy and healthy life. I found a sponsor again and started working the steps. I knew the answers I was looking for were in the steps, Big Book and the meetings. So I poured myself into them.

Slowly, I started putting pieces of my life back together again with help from my sponsor and people from the program. After a few short years, I was working two jobs and trying to pay past bills and child support when I met a lady who would become my third wife. She was not in the program but knew about it. She had twin boys and had just come out of a messy divorce. We lived together for about five years before we got married. During this time, I was going to meetings, working the steps and doing whatever was asked of me.

I then received a call from the mother of my daughter who said she was willing to give me full custody of my daughter. All I needed to do was to go to Baytown and get her. She said she would sign whatever papers were needed. So I went to get my daughter. It was not as easy as it sounded because there was a small matter of my daughter living with another family that her mother had given her away to. I did get my daughter and brought her back to Dallas to live with me. However, the family she was living with was not going to give her up without a fight. So off to court we went and many times I would come back to Dallas exhausted and drained.

They were quick to bring up everything in my past to use against me. I would talk with my sponsor and he would tell me to "just keep the faith" and to trust in the power that had gotten me sober and was keeping me sober. I still had a problem dealing with a "Higher Power" even with the fact I had now been sober for over six years. But I did what I was told. I prayed His will would be done in my daughter's life and He would help me to be able to live with it.

After seven months in court, I was given full custody of my daughter, and I was amazed at the outcome. All I had going for me at the time was doing what was right for her and concentrating on not losing control in the court room. Unknown to me, my sponsor had collected over two dozen letters from people who knew me in the program and I was to give these letters to the court. The letters talked about a man who had come out of the gutter to being a sober member of society, who worked hard for his family, who was always there to help people in the program and who was working each day to be a better person than he was the day before. The night before I had to go back to Houston to go to court, I read these letters. They gave me goose bumps and tears in my eyes. I was still unable to see in myself what others were able to see in me.

In the end, I had my daughter and a chance to make up for the things gone wrong in her life. There were hard times and happy times everyone in the house had to come to terms with. Some of them were easy to work out while others took time. However, in the end my wife and I believed it was best for us to go our separate ways.

Now I was a sober single parent with a teenage daughter. Life became different again. However, I knew as I had learned before that when life changes there are things I can do. I had also learned all I had to do was ask for help from my friends in the program. I did this for all kinds of things, including getting my daughter into school and having a very close female friend explained certain female issues to my daughter that were beyond me. I had learned to trust others.

I would like to say this is how the story stands today, but there were still more changes ahead I needed to face. One was my relationship with God because I still had many issues with that area of my life. In the end, I came to understand it was not God that I was having a problem with, but I found that the problem was with me. God had forgiven me many times over and did great things in my life, but I could not forgive myself. I felt there had to be more to it than just a simple matter of making amends for my past and being a better person today. Then in my 10th year of sobriety I got physically sick. After seeing doctors, I was told I had a serious infection. There was not much I could do except take the pills and wait for the infection to clear up.

It took close to a year before I started to physically heal. Somewhere during my illness, I had lost all faith in myself, the program and what little bit I had in God. So after eleven years of being sober, after all the miracles that happened in my life and in the lives of people around me, I gave up the fight and started drinking again. Deep down inside I knew drinking was not the answer. I also did not live under some idea this time would be different, because I knew it never would be.

During the next few years, I was once again slipping in and out of the program. I was trying to find the desire to stop drinking and things started to change again. I was close to losing my job of twelve years. Furthermore, my daughter, who I loved dearly, came to me one day with tears. She said she knew that she could not stop me from drinking, but she wanted me to know she loved me and always would love me. Her fear was she would have to go live with someone else or that I would end up killing myself. All of this broke my heart and yet I still could not find the will to stop. So time and time again I would go to meetings and pick up a desire chip. I wanted to stay sober. However, time and time again I would be drunk in a few days.

There are no words I know to describe how I felt, needing to drink and knowing there was a better way of life. For me, if there was a hell then this is what it felt like to be there. I have never had this much emotional pain in all my life and the only answer I could come up with was to drink more to make it all go away.

Sometime later, I found myself back in the 12 step rooms. Most of my friends there were afraid they would get the news one day that I was either in jail or dead. I do not know what made this time any different from the times before. However, after being back for only a few weeks, I felt like I should once more start working the steps. At this point, I would have just been happy not to drink, even if nothing else ever changed. Fortunately, I met a guy with 15 years of sobriety and asked him to be my sponsor. He agreed to work with me and gave me a book to read that has turned my understanding about God and my relationship with Him around.

I now understand God really cares about people like me who were lost in the world...people who had lived lives that were not perfect. I know God loves us all. Yet I found he is happy when someone like me can come to trust and believe in Him. I now understood all the things he had done in my life both inside and outside of the program. I learned he not only forgave me but he would also forget the past I had lived. All I needed to do was to forgive myself or, as they say in the program, I needed to "Put the bat down and stop beating myself up." When I did this, my life changed again. Today I have a better understanding of how I fit into God's world. I know I will still make mistakes and when that happens he will not condemn me for them as long as I am trying to make it right and do better the next time around.

It has been close to 3 years now and I have not had a drink. Along the way my life has gotten better. My daughter is going to college and she enjoys spending time with her Dad. I still make meetings every evening and I am also there to help the next person who comes in the door.

Today, I have the life I have seen in others and did not believe I could personally achieve; it is filled with the grace of my God and the love and fellowship of the program, family and friends.

Chapter 40
Desperate Numbness
By: Patti V.

"Girls are closing the gap with boys in terms of usage of marijuana, alcohol and cigarettes. Since 2002, more teenage girls than boys started using marijuana. And in 2004, more girls than boys started using alcohol and cigarettes." [98]

I was born into a family of first generation Americans and immigrants from Mexico and Spain. My parents, like most, did a lot of things right and lots of things not so right. They encouraged us to go to college because they were the first to go to college in their families. They took us on long driving vacations to the Grand Canyon, to Disneyland, and to San Francisco. They gave me and my sister guitar lessons and dance lessons; they bought expensive sneakers for my brother and sent him to sports camps. They wanted better for their children than they had for themselves. There were big gatherings with food, drink and Mexican music with "compadres" and "comadres." Everyone was in everyone's business: a great, animated, enmeshed family where biological lines meant nothing and anyone older than you could be your "aunt" or "uncle."

My parents also had, of course, their faults as human beings and their own immaturities to work out as parents. My mother has a strong tendency towards intense jealousy, envy and judgment when she feels rejected. She also has no sense of emotional boundaries. Now, as an adult and as a therapist, I see it for what it is and know it by its clinical name. As a kid I grew up with a vague but pervasive sense of anxiety, of something being backwards, of having to parent the parent.

When I was 10 my father had an affair and my mother entered what we three kids now label "the crazy years." She dove headfirst into a deep, suicidal depression. She spent hours upon hours crying, screaming into telephones, telling her victim story to anyone who would listen, emotionally vomiting her intense fear and martyrdom on everyone, especially me – the oldest. I have memories of seeing her eyes ringed raccoon-like with running mascara, crying to me, and wanting me to answer her questions and fix her feelings.

When I was 13 she finally moved my sister, brother and me to another city. With relief I thought we were finally moving on in life. Six months later my father followed her and within a few months, he moved back in with us.

At this point, I lost it. I had been treated like the "adult" in the family for too long. I was the "responsible one," and yet I always felt unequipped for the role, like I was a fraud, like I was out on a limb with no support. I was emotionally a child being given adult emotional responsibilities I could not stand it, and I didn't know what to do about it. So I started drinking hard and quickly turned in my "responsible" cape for the label as family "rebel." I got drunk the first time I drank and I loved it. I drank to get drunk *every* time I drank from that point forward.

I discovered marijuana and would spend 45 minutes every morning before school getting high. I would smoke pot at lunch and after school. I would go out anytime I could and get drunk. I remember a family trip skiing when I was 14 years-old where I met a guy on the lift and he turned me on to cocaine and I spent the rest of the weekend going as fast as I possibly could. No turning and no hope of stopping. I was reckless, angry and not caring. I continued living like that for 16 more years.

The irony is that I was always still "the smart one." So even though I skipped school all the time, I made As in all my high school classes. I had a counselor at school that helped me graduate a year early. So at 16, I graduated high school and at 17 had a fully-paid 4 year scholarship to the University of Texas. I held the dream (my mother's dream, really) of going to medical school. Therefore, I enrolled in college and moved out at 17.

But the pace of my personal life didn't allow for inconveniences like studying or going to class. I had always dated older men – 10 and 15 years older. They had money and drugs. I guess I was looking for the dad that was never really there. So I attracted emotionally unavailable addicts who punished me emotionally. Somehow without realizing it, I felt like I needed to be punished. I was not good enough, even though at the time I thought I was just "having fun."

The first guy was a photographer with a critical eye and an even more critical tongue. We did tons of cocaine and hung out at strip clubs where our dealer worked. It was a world of strippers, drugs, pornography, sleeping all day and partying all night. I ignored my family even though they lived in the same city and I completely blew my scholarship by failing out of college. I didn't care.

I left him to be with a bartender with an even more critical eye and an even sharper tongue. With him, I was the child, a role I willingly played. He was uneducated, a speed dealer, obsessive and rigid. I let him be the dominating "daddy" and I shaped myself and my world around him. We moved to Michigan to start a business, moved back to Texas within a year and settled in Dallas. I returned to school and helped him through a 2 year associate's degree. We quit the speed and took up drinking full-time.

I went back to college. However, this time I was determined to get through school. With that nagging sensation that I was never doing it right, was never good enough, and could never achieve enough, I pushed myself relentlessly through college. I graduated cum laude with a Bachelor's in Computer Science. I got a job in telecommunications in 1991. I poured myself into work during the week. I was working harder than anyone else by taking on more responsibilities and more projects. I was recognized and rewarded greatly. Within 3 or 4 years I found myself in positions of heavy responsibility in management. I finally looked on the outside like a "success."

But at home I was the compliant little girl, doing whatever my husband wanted, swallowing my anger, thoughts and feelings before his critical, derogatory and fault-finding personality. I see now he was the judgmental part of my mother magnified a hundred times. I needed someone to disapprove of me, to find fault in me, to punish me. I felt so miserable, not good enough and unworthy on the inside. So I drank more because of these intense feelings I didn't know how to handle, and I desperately tried to run away from in numbness.

I became an intense insomniac and very anxious. I also became suicidal and depressed. I remember sitting in front of my husband at a happy hour, explaining how I felt. He pounded the bar and became angry. I told myself how unsafe it was to tell anyone how I felt and sank further into my depression. I went to my doctor without telling him and started taking antidepressants. I drank more and then alcohol started to fail me. I could drink and drink, but I could not get drunk. I was sick, throwing up and enduring blinding headaches every morning. And I kept drinking harder and faster and the more it didn't work, the more depressed I became. The bleaker my existence, the stronger my suicidal urge became.

I stood literally "at a turning point" and had to decide whether to die or not. And in that moment, exhausted, at an absolute emotional bottom, feeling completely and utterly alone, I gave up. But in that instant between giving up and taking a wrong action, grace fell upon me. Instead of choosing to die, I prayed, "Please help me."

The next day - or maybe that day - I found myself with a stack of books from the library. These were books on alcoholism, addiction and AA. I read for hours about the biochemical and enzymatic reactions of addiction as if knowing this and understanding it could change things. The only thing I remember reading that stuck with me was something that said a true alcoholic ends up dead, in prison or insane. It was the thought of being insane that finally broke me. I felt insane – if there were further depths, I didn't want to go there. I had had it.

I attended my first AA/12 step meeting the next day on my 29th birthday. I remember walking into the smoky room and hearing such compelling honesty and truth. I came back for the recommended 90 meetings in 90 days. After that, I returned for another 90 meetings in 90 days. I found hope in those rooms. I would return to work at my high-pressure, upper management job in Research & Development smelling like a bar room from all the smoke, and I didn't care. The project planning, meetings, customer visits and labs of my career seemed surreal. My house with its baby blue furniture that I didn't realize until after years of sobriety that I hated seemed surreal. My strained relationship with my family seemed surreal. The 1 hour in that smoky 12 step meeting – that was real. I used it as my anchor and I slowly learned who I was.

Three years into sobriety I had "come to" enough to realize how miserable I was in my marriage. I left my first husband and embarked on an incredible journey of living, learning, healing, growing. I met my second husband attended life changing personal growth workshops, and traveled with my job. My relationship with my mother started to heal. Through it all, the 12 step program was my rock, my constant.

I changed groups in 1997 and started attending women's meetings. Previously, I held nothing but contempt for women's meetings. I judged women to be weak, overly emotional, clingy and needy. I saw and judged all women, of course, through the lens of my past. When I started going to the women's meetings at my new club, though, I learned about true friendship and the intimacy that only comes from being with friends through thick and thin. We met for lunch after our 12 step meetings, formed step studies, and attended each others weddings, baby showers, housewarmings and birthday parties. We did service work together. We held each other when marriages failed and talked to each other when temptation threatened our sobriety and relationships. We grew and laughed and learned to trust. With the women, I learned to grow up emotionally and to trust myself and others.

In 2005, I came to another crossroad in my life. I was married again to a wonderful man who didn't understand addiction and had, thankfully, never seen me drunk or high. He respected my sobriety and came to open meetings with me to learn. I was still working ungodly hours and was being groomed for the executive suites. By now, however, I had learned enough about who I was and what I wanted. I decided I needed a vocation, not a career. I left an extremely high-paying job to return to school to get my master's in counseling.

Since then I have worked with at-risk youth, in the psychiatric department of a drug rehab center and in a private practice. I love the work I do. I get paid nothing in comparison to what I made before, but I am happier than I have ever been. I can't make the women's meetings like I used to because I work on Saturdays, but the women from those early days of sobriety remain my rocks, my best friends, my lifelines. I sponsor people actively, attend a step study once a year; and attend 12 step meetings at least once a week. My marriage is strong and committed. I have the healthiest relationship I can with my family given where they are emotionally. I would have none of this without AA and sobriety. I also would not be here without my addiction and everything I went through to get here. So I count myself as one of the thousands who say "I am a grateful recovering addict."

Chapter 41
Unpredictable After Effects
By: Bill H.

"About twice as many women attempt suicide, but men are four times more likely to die from the attempt than the women. Suicide took the lives of over 30,000 Americans, and is the eighth leading cause of death. It is the third leading cause of death for young people ages 15–24 years." [99]

The first drink I remember having was around the age of seven. My grandmother had given me a medicinal ¼ shot of whiskey, and I immediately wanted more. Around the age of 10, I began believing that I was different some how than others. They seemed "whole" while I felt "less than." Much later, I heard a 12 step speaker finally describe my feelings: I felt like swiss cheese on the inside and alcohol filled the holes to make me feel whole.

My first drunk occurred when I was 13 years old. I was home after my parents went out. They had left their and another couples' partially drank cocktails in the kitchen sink. I mixed them all into one glass and went to watch T.V. I remember drinking the cocktail and afterwards the T.V. began to slowly spin sideways. After finishing the drink, I was unable to walk and I crawled upstairs to bed. I thought, "WOW! What a cool feeling getting drunk was." It had changed my perception of life for a short while and was ready to do it again soon.

When I entered high school, I partied on the weekends and during my senior year moved from a small suburb south of Cleveland, Ohio to Dallas, Texas. What a culture shock! The kids dressed slick, drove fancy cars, and were extremely intelligent (the school was rated in the nation's top schools several years in a row.) I really felt out of place but, by mid-October of 1977, I found my way to fit in: DRINKING. Alcohol removed my inhibitions; made me feel whole and made me feel a part of the activities around me. I was proud to say drinking is what I did best. There were not many that could keep up with the "Tequila Kid" or "Mad Dog Man." Both my nicknames were acquired because of the amount of alcohol that I could consume. At the time, I was proud of my titles because no one could drink like me!

After I graduated high school in 1978, my family moved to St. Louis, Missouri. Again I was lost because I knew no one; I had no idea what to make of my life; I did not know what direction to follow; and I did not know what to do when I grew up. I had attended one semester of college back in Texas, but unfortunately, I did not get much out of it. This is mainly because when a person is drinking 4 or 5 days a week college and homework are not on the top of their agenda. I decided I would not go to college the next semester. Instead, I worked a full-time job and also a part-time job. I could not decide what I wanted to do for a career.

Two weeks before leaving to go to Missouri College, I went out drinking and received my first of two driving drunk arrests. I vaguely remember coming in and out of a blackout in the back of the squad car. I made the cops angry when I somehow got my hands from behind me to my front by sliding them under my feet. They also did not find it humorous when I told the mug shot photographer to "hold on a sec" while I combed my hair.

I went to college and, to appease my parents, I also went to a couple of Alcoholics Anonymous (AA-12 step) meetings. I went to the meetings did not pay much attention. After listening to the other alcoholics talking, I thought to myself, "I am NOT THAT BAD I just got caught."

For awhile, at school I did not do any partying. The only thing I did was study and I had a 4.0 average after ¾ of a semester. During spring break, I had to go to court for my DWI and I was scared. The judge sentenced me to an alcohol awareness class and harshly explained that he had better NEVER see me in his court room again. Not only was court expensive, but the alcohol awareness class was too. I was not happy when the addiction counselor told my parents that I was coasting through and strongly recommended I also take the 2nd alcohol class. I did not end with a 4.0 that semester. After my court date, I decided that I had my grades licked and started partying again on the weekends. This eventually led to the week days and left no time for studying.

I went to college for another two semesters while drinking harder and harder. I was offered an opportunity to enter a Store Management Training Program for the company that I was working for during the summer. I started the 18 month training program and was promoted to store manager within 9 months. I was still drinking heavily and I was working non-stop.

I consider July 4th, 1982, to be the beginning of the end of my drinking. I had one of my classic blackout episodes (AGAIN), and I made a complete fool of myself. I was rarely a "get drunk and pass out drinker." I would have blackouts and completely function throughout the night. The problem was I did not have any recollection the next day, and I would do regrettable things during the blackouts that I would never have done sober.

Labor Day weekend of 1982, was the finale of my drinking career. Once again, I made a drunken fool of myself, but this time it was at my girlfriend's parents' home. I humiliated myself and I did not know how I would ever face them again.

After the holiday, I returned to work and found I could not do the daily report for the store sales because my hands and body were shaking so badly. This was the beginning signs of the Delirium Tremors or DTs. Since I figured I just needed to calm down after a bad weekend, I wrote myself a prescription and began to take 10 mg. of Valium. It worked temporarily and I finished the report before the employees got to the store.

I barely remember the last two weeks of my drinking. I was consuming as much alcohol as I could, approximately 750 ml while taking between 5000 mg to 10,000 mg of Valium per day. I did this continuously for two solid weeks.

It is important I explain how I felt about myself at the time. Now, after so many years I can put labels on them. I did not have the ability to do this when I was using and first getting sober. I was egotistical to make up for my feelings of low self-esteem. I felt lonely and unlovable; that I was a loser. I was fearful of the past, present and future. I also felt underutilized and unappreciated at work. I considered myself an unlucky worrier and a self-centered big dreamer. I had an inferiority complex and I was depressed. I felt my life was better living drunk, but I could not any longer stand the after effects and unpredictable behavior while I was drinking. I considered myself to be an agnostic and I knew I was going to lose the girl of my dreams.

On the 16th of September I was pulled over again for driving while intoxicated, but I was not jailed this time. I remember waking up in the court house waiting room not knowing where I was or what was happening. During first DWI, I blew a .28 in the breathalyzer machine. The officers did not believe the results of my second DWI, and they took me to the county hospital for a blood test. (I was in a blackout and do not remember any of this.) The blood test came back a .42 and showed how quickly I slid down the slope of alcoholism. I was not put in a jail cell because the officers wanted to monitor me because they were afraid I might die from alcohol poisoning. The legal amount of alcohol permitted in a person's blood is .08 in most states.

By September 18th, I was a basket case. My mother found a bottle of pills I had hidden and asked me what they were for. I lied and told her I did not know. I then remember quickly downing all the remaining pills in the bottle. The next memory I have was being in the Emergency Room and getting my stomach pumped. I had not eaten in two days so the pills had digested fast, but I was still alive.

After my suicide attempt, I was taken into a lady's office at the hospital and she told me I had three choices and I better make the right one. The *first choice* was to go to the psyche ward on the fourth floor of the hospital. The *second choice* was to go home and continue my life as before. The *third option* was to go to a place called Edgewood and it would give me a reprieve from the courts, work and responsibilities. They would show me a new way of life based on a 12 step program.

This was my FIRST SPIRITUAL EXPERIENCE, for some untold reason God spoke through me and said my choice was "Door number three, Monty I'll take Edgewood."

I spent two weeks in ICU detoxifying and was given an anti-psychotic drug treatment because I was seeing weird scary things on the walls. My next four weeks were spent doing the first 8 steps. My SECOND SPIRITUAL EXPERIENCE was during my third week when I realized I would not have to drink or use drugs again by living and working the 12 steps.

I was given a temporary sponsor who I began to call while I was in treatment. It was explained to me to get involved with the 12 steps and to follow the instructions or I would go back to my old lifestyle. I believe an alcoholic in treatment who goes back to drinking will end up in one of the following ways: 1.) In prison; 2.) Institutionalized; or 3.) Dead. I was scared to leave the safety of the hospital, but I finally did with the help of my girlfriend and family.

One of the main points I remember about treatment are the statistics they told me. I thought were staggering such as 1 in 20 will make it to 5 years; 1 in 40 would still be sober in 10 years; and 1 in 100 would make it to 20 years of sobriety. (These stats may not have been proven in any study, but it was the treatment center's experience.) The people who would remain sober would get a sponsor and stick close to them, get a home group and attend weekly meetings, get involved in 12 step activities, work the steps, hang out with sober friends and drop the old ones. The theory remains *if you walk like a duck and talk like a duck - then you are a duck!*

Four weeks after leaving treatment, I had my court appointment for my second DWI. I had the same presiding judge, who said he never wanted to see me in his court again. After he was told I had been to treatment, he was lenient with me and said I would need to have a paper signed at 12 step meetings for 6 months. I was to give the sheets to a parole officer every month. Thus, I attended meetings every day and sometimes twice a day. I really wanted to change and did not want go back to the way I was before treatment. The DWI was ultimately released from my record. Three years later, I made an amends to the judge when I saw his name on a re-election ballet and I voted for him.

I went back to work with a demotion and worked hard to get back my old position, but I lost the job eventually. I was not changing myself inside and was again falling into an emotional black hole. God was the only one I could talk to. I tried repeatedly to talk to my sponsor about feeling good, bad and indifferent, but I could not express myself. The words would not come out. I now know it was my EGO keeping me from doing so; it kept telling me, "Don't become vulnerable!"

After my ninth month of sobriety many of my friends with longer sobriety than I had began having all sorts of troubles and tribulations. I wondered if what I was doing was really worth it and was pondering what to do next. I began putting on a façade that everything was FINE (this really means Fu*%ed up, Insecure, Neurotic, Emotional) with me but internally I was spiraling down an emotional black hole. I began changing everything around me instead of myself. As a result, I had lost my job, my girlfriend and my self-respect. I threw myself harder into the 12 steps by going to two meetings a day and getting involved in a convention that was in St. Louis. But I was still not able to focus on the problem…ME. I just avoided it. Drinking was not an option to go back to, so the pain and suffering of suicide became my option.

I planned out my suicide carefully. I went to my parents' secluded river cabin in the country to carry out my plan. It consisted of buying records to listen to; taking 100 aspirin to thin my blood; mixing a toxic poisonous gas with bleach and chlorine; and slicing both wrists with a carpet cutter. I was following through with my plan when I passed out. Before awaking I felt a peace I had never felt before and I heard a voice say, "You'll be okay."

After waking, I immediately left the cabin and drove to my sponsor's house. He was not there so I went to another friend's home who was also in the 12 step program. When she opened the door and saw me she said, "Don't you know God does NOT make junk?" I collapsed on the couch. The next thing I knew, I was in the psyche hospital. I spent the next six weeks there and learned more about myself; I learned how to ask for help and how to talk about things I could not talk about before.

After leaving the hospital, I attended a weekly video tape talk session called the "Dog and Pony Show of Joe and Charlie." I learned more about the disease of alcoholism including the alcohol break down process and the effects on the body. My sponsor suggested that I learn more about the 12 steps so I studied. I also started studying the Big Book of AA instead of just reading it.

In January of 1985, I went back to college to earn my degree. I worked full-time, went to school full-time and went to meetings at least 3 to 4 times a week. I began to learn how to relax and have fun. Before getting sober, I would go fishing to catch fish, but now I was learning to relax and simply enjoy the beauty of nature.

I graduated from college in January of 1989, and I got a job with a company whose owner was familiar with the program. I learned about business first-hand and started my sales career. I love to sell! Part of my job was traveling around the Midwest and I would go to meetings in other cities and states. I met some great friends during this time who are still friends of mine today. Many of these friends are "normies" better known as "earth people" or non-alcoholics. After three years of working there, I moved back to Dallas to take another job.

I moved again from St. Louis to Dallas. In Dallas, I had to start over and make new friends, attend new meetings, find a new home group and secure a new sponsor. Though the meetings formats were different, the common bond of recovery joined us together.

With about 12 years of sobriety, a customer of mine introduced me to Jujitsu and Japanese Sword. I spent 6 years rigorously practicing and getting my black belt. They became my passion. I eventually hurt my lower back and the surgeon told me I needed to stop. So I began a quest to find what else I could do to stay in shape and have fun.

The Olympics were on T.V. and I saw fencing; and I thought to myself, "I could do that!" After back surgery and being released from my surgeon's care, I looked into fencing through the Parks and Recreation Center where I live. I signed up for the classes thinking it would be easy since I had been in Japanese swords for so long. It was not! The foot work and the muscle groups that I had to use were totally different. But I hung in there and kept practicing and practicing. Fencing became my new passion. I competed in the National tournament and placed in the top 32 in my age group.

I am now about 6 weeks from my 25th sobriety birthday and I compete in Foil and Epee. I have replaced my drinking and drugging with a healthy sport that I love just as much as I loved my alcohol and drugs. Though I will not win a spot on the Olympic Team, I do plan on being able to make the team for the Veterans World Finals in a few years, when I am eligible.

I help teach the beginning fencers class and the adult class through our fencing club. A year ago, I volunteered to help our coach with the wheel chair fencing class, which is a humbling and gratifying experience.

As the "Big Book" of Alcoholics Anonymous says in the promises, *"May we meet while trudging the happy road of destiny and may God bless you and keep you in the palm of His hand."*

Chapter 42
President of the Psych Ward
By: Sandy M.

"Never married, divorced and separated women generally have the highest rates of heavy drinking and drinking related problems." [100]

I was reared in a small oilfield town where I was always encouraged to have more ambition – and success – than my neighbors. Since my dad was my high school principal, I always felt it necessary to "appear" to be perfect. Mother and Daddy were very active in the church and saw to it that we attended every time the door was open. This background supported my inborn trait of perfectionism and my habit of scanning the environment to see where I fit in. I was either better than or worse than everyone I analyzed. I had no sense of being a peer and no understanding that everyone is perfect just the way they are. Alternately, I thought that the whole world should be like me. I also thought if I could only find "the answer" then my life would play out in a most wonderful way and I would never have to struggle again. I would continue to believe that for thirty-nine years.

I met and married the love of my life in college. When I graduated I taught school so that he could get his doctorate degree. We worked hard for six years and saw each other very little due to our demanding schedules. I guess I bought into the theory that to succeed you have to work very hard, make great sacrifices, and hardly ever be at home. While this is true to some extent, but there are limits - limits that I didn't recognize because of my strong sense of denial and ability to "push through."

Shortly after my second daughter was born, my oldest one was diagnosed with severe asthma. She was hospitalized for a week at a time every month or so. I had to give up breast feeding my baby at nine months because my oldest daughter was sick so often. The hospitalizations caused me to be away from her for long periods of time. It was around this time I discovered that my husband was gay. I stayed in that marriage for nine more years never telling anyone of my sorrow except for my gynecologist who suggested that I remain in the marriage since I wouldn't be able to hold down a job with two children under two and a half, one of whom was chronically ill. After much thought, we were finally divorced.

I was forced by a series of unfortunate events to realize I had to make a decision about my life. I was no longer able to look the other way when my husband was out of town or when he didn't come home until very late at night. I began drinking to take the pain away. I drank only after my daughters were in bed and I was always at home. The result was few could pick up on the fact I had a problem with alcohol, and I had no social consequences that might have aroused any attention.

Eventually my drinking became such a problem that a good friend of mine, who was a counselor, suggested I check myself into a local hospital for evaluation. She suggested that it might take only a couple of days or so. Fifty-two days later, I walked out of the hospital having spent the most bizarre, but important, two months of my life. I had been in the "psych" ward and witnessed all sorts of mental illness. There was a young lady who stared into space and rocked back and forth. There was a man restrained in a straight-jacket shouting obscenities around the clock. There were several who attempted suicide. All of this was very different from my middle class suburban life where the talk focused on social/volunteer work, our husbands' jobs, and our children's futures. One funny memory was being elected president of the "psych" ward. I wondered if it would help me develop my resume which had just become a sobering problem for me.

That hospital stay was part of a divine plan. I was assigned to a psychiatrist who had five years' recovery in Alcoholics Anonymous. He suggested I look at my drinking. My thoughts, of course, were that you'd drink, too, if you'd been through what I've been through for the last nine years. He took me to a meeting and encouraged me to read the Big Book. When he asked me what I thought about my reading, I replied, "It's not written very well." Such was my denial!

I did begin going to 12 step meetings every day, and I was convinced I needed to have them as a priority while going back to graduate school to prepare for a career change. I was very concerned about my children who were now in elementary school. I was convinced I had to commit to my sobriety before anything else. Everything else would then fall into place.

I got my masters degree and changed career fields. Once again divine guidance led me to a job which fit my needs and lifestyle very well.

I remarried after two years. I married a very fine man with five years sobriety. He was a professional and seemed to be the answer to all my problems.

Things began to be stressful when my six year-old niece was diagnosed with and died from Leukemia in the next years. At that point, I had to make sense of this tragedy. I needed to decide how this fit into my belief system and how my world would be different from then on. My husband was very conservative and couldn't abide my seeking. I began to realize the very reasons I married him (conservative, I'd always know where he was and that he was faithful, hard-working and no-nonsense) were the same reasons why I would be unable to sustain the marriage. We divorced. He has since married a lovely lady who goes to his church and is as conservative as he is. They have a wonderful marriage.

I dated another man in AA, who was also a wonderful person. We dated for the most part – alcoholics tend to break up and go back to each other often – of 10 years. We finally married. He wanted to be married and I didn't want to grow old alone. I knew we had major differences, but I thought being good people and having the 12 step program in common would see us through. No marriage is perfect. During this time (seventeen years in all) I was caring for my elderly parents and watching them slip away from me bit by bit. My life began to turn gray – not much joy and too little laughter. I began to play computer games and to wonder what life might have been like if I had married my high school sweetheart. As luck would have it, my high school sweetheart contacted me through a web site for high school alumni. He lived in one of the suburbs near mine.

I began to remember what it was like to have someone's eyes light up when I came into the room and to be aware I was the person that my high school sweetheart would choose over everyone else in the world to be with. This was very seductive when I looked at my life which felt like cardboard. We began to e-mail and to have lunch. We had an affair, but it was one of the heart. He was a very ill man; he had Chronic Obstructive Pulmonary Disease and other accompanying other ailments.

My husband discovered that we were seeing each other and rightly wanted a divorce. I think I subconsciously wanted one, too. I do know I wanted to quit hurting and mourning.

My husband moved out and I had to refinance the house to pay him his part. The next month my mother had another stroke on a Friday. My dad fell and broke his other hip on the next Friday. The next Friday he had a long-shot surgery. The next Friday he died. So now I was going through a divorce, trying to get the house settled, my dad had died and my mother's condition began to deteriorate.

My mother died a year after my dad. My high school sweetheart died a week after Mother. I lost two aunts in the following two months and in January my last remaining uncle wandered away from his assisted living arrangement and froze to death. They couldn't readily find his body so they called in a helicopter; he had on khaki clothes that blended into the dead grass. My cousin, my uncle's son, helped search for him and had a heart attack when they found him. We had to delay the funeral for two weeks to see if my cousin would live and could go to the funeral.

I went through many feelings over all of these events that occurred so close together. I always had the help of my 12 step meetings and the wonderful ladies I had bonded with over the 23 years since I first began my trek on my road to happy destiny.

I have a wonderful sponsor and I also sponsor several beautiful ladies. I pointed out these trials because I now know that it's while I'm going through my greatest difficulties that I grow the most. After making it through another challenge, I could look back and see the divine guidance and provisions given me. I have witnessed my friends go through as many difficult, if not more difficult, times as I have, and we have a connection that cannot be gained by any other way than remaining teachable and seeking the blessings of Life.

Today I feel like a different person. I feel so blessed. Most days are filled with peace and joy; all of my days are filled with gratitude for a beautiful life. I never lose touch with the gifts the 12 steps have given me. As the program promises, I truly have had a psychic change.

Chapter 43
In Shame I Found My Gifts
By: Michelle M.

Studies show that more than 35% of adults with an alcohol problem developed symptoms—such as binge drinking—by age 19. [101]

Hello! My name is Michelle. I am a believer in Jesus Christ who has been clean and sober from drugs and alcohol since March 5th of 1997 only by the grace of a loving and merciful God. As I share with you, please know the things I share are not to glamorize or glorify my drug and alcohol use or the life I lead. It is only to identify me as a recovering addict/alcoholic and bring hope to you so you can go through or do the things I have done and still sober up because you are a child of God and worthy of his love.

I was born the third daughter of my father and the second to my mother. I was followed a year later with a younger brother. I was raised in Houston, Texas. I lived in the same house from the age of two and went to the same schools my older sister and younger brother attended. My parents were both Christians and I attended church in my younger years. We went to vacation bible school and Baptist church camp. I walked the aisle and was baptized. By all accounts, my life should have turned out different than it did. At some point though, between children's church and "Big" church thing changed. I crossed the breezeway of that Baptist church and God changed from "Jesus loves me," rainbows, and fuzzy bunnies to a mean, condemning God who was going to get me. But I have come to realize that really did not happen. I started living a life not pleasing to God and turned from him. He never left me. In fact, had God not been with me I would not have survived the path I took for the balance of my childhood and well into my adulthood.

Unfortunate situations happened to me throughout my childhood and my parents were unaware of them until I was a grown woman. This did not cause my alcoholism and addiction. Neither did anything my parents did or did not do. I made choices along the way to live a life that lead me away from God. However, I do believe today everything I have been through - every mistake I made every breath I have taken, everything I have ever gone through - has made me the woman I am today. My biggest mistakes, pains, and shame have become gifts I can give to other women that do not see any way out.

I started with the medicine cabinet at home and quickly moved to those of my friends' parents. Alcohol seemed to fill the hole in my gut. It took me away. I was tall, beautiful and had no cares when I drank. It did not last forever though, since most of the time I could not remember what I had done. I ran with kids whose parents were divorced and did not care what they did. But my parents asked many questions and did care what I was up to, but this did not stop me. I blended into whatever group I was with – goodies, kickers, freaks, or jocks were all included in the circles I traveled. No one knew who I really was – including me.

I used every drug available every way there was to do it. Since I drank as an alcoholic from the beginning, my drinking did not change. I blew relationships and, as mentioned previously, had very few "friends" who really knew me. When I received my first DWI my parents helped me get a deferred adjudication which resulted in few consequences and only seemed like a slap on the wrist. I continued to go out and not know how I got home – if I made it home. I did what I had to do to drink and drug.

I met the man who would become my first husband and we moved in together. We had a beautiful little boy and started raising him. Amazingly still loves me and even shares his children with me. I quit my job to stay home and take care of the children in the home. He was part owner of his family's wrecker service business. However, he really did not like working, so we started selling the drugs we were using. The relationship was abusive - especially after a night of heavy drinking or a several day drug run. We were married when my son was four; however, the marriage was killed and ended because of drug and alcohol abuse by the time he was seven. Of course, the job I had taken in a bar had nothing to do with it – or so that is what I told myself. I convinced myself that my marriage and my husband were my problems and if I could just get out of Houston my life was going to change and get better. I thought a geographical change was the answer. I did give up IV drug use but despite my promise to myself, sobriety eluded me.

I moved to Dallas, Texas, to live with a wonderful Christian aunt after securing a job there. That was February of 1986 and by March I was drinking again. I joined a church, got involved with the singles group, rededicated my life and was baptized. I thought this would work. I even saw a counselor in the church who assured me I was a situational drinker and I would be okay. I used that as a seal of approval to continue to drink. It did not take me long to start using drugs again. I told myself it was okay since I was only snorting it or taking pills. I eventually felt too much shame and guilt to sit in church on Sunday morning. As hard as I tried, as much as I prayed, I never felt the same way the other women in church did. They were beautiful shiny women who sang in the choir. Their eyes always seemed to have a light I never could feel inside. I felt dirty and unworthy, like I was not good enough to be there. I had spent most of my life measuring my insides by others outsides. I eventually just disappeared again into a world of work, alcohol, drugs and eventually another on-again/off-again relationship leading to a very short marriage. The second marriage was just as damaging to both of us as my first one and it did not make me feel loved or cared for. I used relationships to try and fill up a bottomless pit I seemed to have inside of me. Before the annulment was final I had met my future husband number three. During this time, my father and brother had bouts with the law and both were sent to prison. The fact my husband was on parole did not send up red flags that he may end up there also.

I had miraculously kept the same job I had taken when I moved to Dallas, and I now had taken a part-time job in a bar to pay for classes I enrolled in. Chaos! I met Richard, my last husband, at my part-time job. After a short time, we moved in together. Eventually I left the part-time job and did not return to school the next semester. The company I for whom I had worked for nine years was closing its retail division, and I had to find a new job. During this time I went to work for a company I would stay with for the next almost 10 years. Over the next several years, Richard and I tried to kill ourselves with our drinking and drugging. We were married and four years later after several separations and reconciliations our marriage ended with the same fate my first one had. I left when I found him shooting cocaine. I knew if I did not leave I would start shooting again and I did not want to. Once again, I was sure that if I got out of that marriage I could get clean and sober.

My brother was out of prison and sober. I had spent half of my adult life taking him to meetings and trying to help him get sober. I had never once done that for myself. I had always felt guilty because my first husband and I had sold my brother the very drugs he got hooked on. His life was changing – getting better. I sought out counseling via my sober brother and his sponsor who also recommended an Alanon meeting. I did not make it to the Alanon meeting until recently.

My last drink was on March 4th 1997. For some reason, I just could not do it anymore. I could not live the way I was living or do the things I had been doing one more day of my life. This was not my first "Aha" moment God had given me. It was simply the first one to which I paid attention. My father came home in February and I spent the next three years as a sober daughter. I made amends to my son for all I had put him through. Since he also had his own issues with drugs and alcohol, he eventually went to prison on drug-related issues for a short stint. Sadly, he was introduced to his first daughter through the glass at Harris County Jail when I was there for a meeting. I am happy to say for the last ten years, I have been there as a sober mother and grandmother.

As far as the meeting, I showed up for what I thought was an Alanon meeting which actually turned out to be an AA meeting. It has always been a joke because I think my therapist really tricked me into AA. It turned out that she and my first sponsor knew each other. My sponsor took me through the steps and helped me to understand God still loved me no matter what I had done or been - God was there for me even when I was unaware of it.

My father died in 2000. My AA family and my childhood friends were there for me. The best part was I was able to be there for my family. I continue to be there for my family by staying clean and sober. I maintain a household to provide a home for my 70 year-old mother. My mother was always supported me and watched me struggle throughout my life and loved me through it all.

Richard, my last husband, went back to prison in August of 1997. Unfortunately, he saw no other way out and hung himself in his jail cell on February 3, 2000. This was the same day my father had his aneurysm. My AA family once again rallied and walked me through the guilt and pain.

I am working for a company I have been with for the last four years. There are some challenges, but usually the common denominator of my problems is of my own making. I am glad to say that I went back to school after my last divorce. The "MRS." degree was not working for me. I worked hard and received my associate degree in 2004. I am currently working on my 4 year degree.

I did a lot of volunteer work recommended by my first sponsor and it brought about tremendous healing. To help heal myself because of my abusive marriages, I volunteered with Genesis Women's Shelter. For my grief over my son's path, I worked with first time offenders through Dallas County Juvenile. I have served on the board for two different women's recovery homes, one which houses women coming straight from the penitentiary. I have served on a team that takes AA meetings to the women's prisons in Gatesville, Texas for the last seven or eight years. I am sponsored by a woman who takes sponsorship seriously and is also sponsored. We have been working together for the last eight years.

As far as relationships, I have not found it necessary to get married since May 1997 - when my last divorce was final. I have spent the last ten years trying to learn who I am and what it is God has planned for me. You see, I had never asked God to lead me to the person he had in mind for me – the partner he prepared for me. In the past, I always chose a broken relationship and then begged God to fix it. I have seen someone off and on for the last ten years and he is as broken as I am in the area of relationships. A couple of years ago when he asked me to marry him I said no. For the first time, I wanted more.

My most important recent decision was to get back involved with a strong church home. My mother moved here and had been attending a church in Houston. She wanted to find a similar church. I had not been to church in a very long time. I had worked on a spiritual life, but I knew in my heart I needed and wanted more. It was God working in my life. In February of this year, we joined a large church and attended a great class that the great Zig Ziglar himself hosted. While at the orientation for new members, I was blessed to meet a singles minister and our conversation turned to recovery. I continued to stay in touch about a recovery program in the church. When the opportunity evolved, I was very excited but a little afraid. I am not strong in scripture, but I can offer my experience, strength and hope about recovery and sobriety. I am willing to learn. Being teachable will continue to be the key for me to achieve a better life through my Higher Power, Jesus Christ.

Section V

Help is Available

"It is never too late to be what you might have been."

– George Eliott

HELP IS AVAILABLE...

Adult Children of Alcoholics

A Twelve Step program of women and men who grew up in alcoholic or otherwise dysfunctional homes who meet to find freedom from the past and ways to improve today
www.adultchildrenofalcoholics.org
310-534-1815

Al-Anon

Whether the alcoholic is still drinking or not, Al-Anon offers hope and recovery to all people affected by the alcoholism of a loved one or friend. Friends and families are welcome. This group uses the 12 step program for recovery.
www.al-anon.alateen.org
1-888-425-2666

Alateen

Whether the alcoholic is still drinking or not, Alateen offers hope and recovery to teenagers and children affected by the alcoholism of a loved one or friend. Friends and families are welcome. This group uses the 12 step program for recovery.
www.al-anon.alateen.org
1-888-425-2666

Alcoholics Anonymous (AA)

An international fellowship of men and women who have had a drinking problem; it is nonprofessional, self-supporting, nondenominational, multiracial, apolitical, self-help group open to anyone who wants to do something about their drinking problem. This group uses the 12 step program of recovery.
www.aa.org
(212) 870-3400

Alcohólicos Anónimos (AA)

Alcoholics Anonymous' outreach and support for speakers of Spanish. An international fellowship of men and women who have had a drinking problem; it is nonprofessional, self-supporting, nondenominational, multiracial, apolitical, self-help group open to anyone who wants to do something about their drinking problem. This group uses the 12 step program of recovery.
http://www.aa.org/sp_information_aa.cfm
(212) 870-3400

Cocaine Anonymous (CA)

A fellowship of men and women who share their experience, strength and hope with each other so that they may solve their common problem and help others to recover from their addiction; the primary purpose is to stay free from cocaine and all other mind-altering substances, and to help others achieve the same freedom. This group uses the 12 step program of recovery.
www.ca.org
310-559-5833

Dual Recovery Anonymous (DRA)

An independent, twelve-step, self-help organization for people with a dual diagnosis of chemically dependence and an emotional or psychiatric illness. Addresses how both illnesses affect all areas of life. This group uses the 12 step program of recovery.
www.draonline.org
1-877-883-2332

Gamblers Anonymous (GA)

An international fellowship of men and women who have had a gambling problem; it is nonprofessional, self-supporting, nondenominational, multiracial, apolitical, self-help group open to anyone who wants to do something about their gambling problem. This group uses the 12 step program of recovery.
www.gamblersanonymous.org
(213) 386-8789

Nicotine Anonymous (NicA)

A fellowship of men and women who have had a smoking problem and want to live nicotine free; it is nonprofessional, self-supporting, nondenominational, multiracial, apolitical, self-help group open to anyone who wants to do something about their smoking and nicotine problem. This group uses the 12 step program of recovery.
www.nicotine-anonymous.org
(415) 750-0328

Narcotics Anonymous (NA)

An international fellowship of men and women who have had a drug problem; it is nonprofessional, self-supporting, nondenominational, multiracial, apolitical, self-help group open to anyone who wants to do something about their drug problem. This group uses the 12 step program of recovery.
www.na.org
1-818-773-9999

Nar-Anon Family Groups

Nar-Anon is a twelve-step program designed to help relatives and friends of addicts recover from the effects of living with an addicted relative or friend. This group uses the 12 step program of recovery.
www.nar-anon.org
310) 534-8188 or 1-800-477-6291

Overeaters Anonymous (OA)

Is a twelve-step program for people identifying themselves as "powerless over food" including, but not limited to, compulsive overeaters, those with binge eating disorder, bulimics and anorexics. This group uses the 12 step program of recovery.
www.oa.org
505-891-2664

Sex and Love Addicts Anonymous (SLAA)

A fellowship of men and women who have a problem with sex addiction and love addiction; it is nonprofessional, self-supporting, nondenominational, multiracial, apolitical, self-help group open to anyone who wants to do something about their sex and love addictions. This group uses the 12 step program of recovery.
www.slaafws.org
210-828-7900

Residential Treatment Houses

Oxford House

Nonprofit organization which connects all Oxford Houses and allocates resources to duplicate the Oxford House concept where need arises. The concept describes a democratically run, self-supporting and drug free group home.
www.oxfordhouse.org
301-587-2916 or 1-800-689-6411

Phoenix House

Nonprofit organization devoted to the treatment and prevention of substance abuse; treats nearly 5,400 adults and adolescents each day at more than 80 programs in eight states. www.phoenixhouse.org
1-800-HELP111

Books for the Latest Research Information

The Science of Addiction, by Carlton K. Erickson, PhD
Erickson, C.K., Science of Addiction: From Neurobiology to Treatment, W.W. Norton, New York, NY (2007).

This is an in-depth source for the latest scientific research information on alcoholism and drug addiction. It explains scientifically in-depth and up-to-date knowledge on the topic.

References

1. "Substance Abuse: The Nation's Number One Health Problem," Institute for Health Policy, Brandeis University, 2001. http://www.ncadd.org/facts/numberoneprob.html

2. Bridget F. Grant, Ph.D., and Deborah A. Dawson, PhD., NIAAA's Division f Biometry and Epidemiology, Journal of Substance Abuse and based on the NIAAA-sponsored National Longitudinal Alcohol Epidemiologic Survey (NLAES). January 1995. http://www.girlpower.gov/press/research/age.htm

3. Position Paper on Drug Policy, Physician Leadership on National Drug Policy (PLNDP), Brown University Center for Alcohol and Addiction Studies, 2000. http://www.ncadd.org/facts/numberoneprob.html

4. "Teen Drug Use" Statistics on Teenage Drug Use. Teen Help LLC. http://www.teendrugabuse.us/teen_drug_use.html

5. NIAA Brochure. "About.com Alcoholism a Widespread Problem," Alcohol Getting the Facts. November 2003. http://alcoholism.about.com/cs/homework/a/blproblem.htm

6. "Substance Abuse: The Nation's Number One Health Problem," Institute for Health Policy, Brandeis University, 2001. http://www.ncadd.org/facts/numberoneprob.html

7. "AboutAlcoholicsAnonymous"The Early History ofAlcoholics Anonymous. Integrity Business Systems and Solutions. http://www.about-alcoholics-anonymous.com

8. "Women and Drug Abuse," NIDA Capsules 6/94, http://www.ncadd.org/facts/women.html

9. "Alcoholics Information" Statistics on Alcoholics. Alcoholics Info. http://www.alcoholics-info.com/statistics_on_alcoholics.html

10. "Teen Drug Use" Statistics on Teenage Drug Use. Teen Help LLC. http://www.teendrugabuse.us/teen_drug_use.html

11. "Drinking in the United States" Main Findings from the 1992 National Longitudinal Alcohol Epidemiologic Survey, National Institute on Alcohol Abuse and Alcoholism, 11/98. http://www.ncadd.org/facts/fyidina.html

12. "About.com: Alcoholism," Drug Users: Young Drug Users Brain Similar to Alzheimer's, 2006. http://alcoholism.about.com/od/sa/a/blue050621.htm

13. "Teen Drug Use" Statistics on Teenage Drug Use. Teen Help LLC. http://www.teendrugabuse.us/teendrugstatistics.html

14. Ibid.

15. "Teen Drug Use" Statistics on Teenage Drug Use. Teen Help LLC. http://www.teendrugabuse.us/teen_drug_use.html

16. Foster, S.E. Vaughn, R.D. Foster, W.H. & Califano, J.A. (2003). Alcohol Consumption and Expenditures for Underage Drinking and Adult Excessive Drinking. JAMA. 289: 989-995. http://www.cspinet.org/booze/030904NASTP.htm

17. National Survey of Substance Abuse Attitudes, Feb. 2001. http://www.gdcada.org/statistics/teens.htm

18. Substance Abuse and Mental Health Services Administration. 2001 National Household Survey on Drug Abuse: Volume II. Technical Appendices and Selected Data Tables, last referenced 5/28/03. http://family.samhsa.gov/talk/illegaldrug.aspx

19. National Highway Traffic Safety Administration. Impaired Driving in the United States. Incidences of Impaired Driving. Pacific Institute for Research and Evaluation, 2000. http://www.nhtsa.dot.gov/people/injury/alcohol/impaired_driving_pg2/us.htm

20. M. McCaul & J. Furst, "Alcoholism Treatment in the United States," AHRW, Vol. 18, No. 4, 1994, pg 257. http://www.ncadd.org/facts/women.html

21. Office of Applied Studies. (2003). "Results from the 2002 National Survey on Drug Use and Health" National findings (DHHS Publication No. SMA 03-3836, NHSDA Series H-22). Rockville, MD: Substance Abuse and Mental Health Services Administration. http://www.drugabusestatistics.samhsa.gov/2k3/drugdriving/drugdribing.htm

22. "Teen Drug Use" Statistics on Teenage Drug Use. Teen Help LLC. http://www.teendrugabuse.us/teen_drug_use.html

23. Journal of the American Medical Association news release, 3/12/96. http://www.ncadd.org/facts/women.html

24. "Teen Substance Abuse" Teen Statistics. Greater Dallas Council on Alcoholism and Drug Abuse. March 2006. http://www.gdcada.org/statistics/teens.htm

25. University of Michigan, Monitoring the Future National Results on Adolescent Drug Use: Overview of Key Findings 2005, April 2006. http://www.jp.usdoj.gov/bjs/dcf/du.htm

26. "Cocaine Statistics and Resources" Short Term Effects. Greater Dallas Council on Alcoholism and Drug Abuse. March 2005. http://www.gdcada.org/statistics/cocaine/stat.htm

27. Collins & P Messerschmidt, "Epidemiology of Alcohol-Related Violence," AHRW, Vol. 17, No. 2, 1993, p. 96. http://www.ncadd.org/facts/women.html

28. U.S. Department of Health and Human Services. Substance Abuse and Mental Health Services Administration. (2002, September 4). Results from the 2001 National Household Survey on Drug Abuse: Volume 1 Summary from the National Findings. http://oas.samhsa.gov/nhsda/2k1nhsda/vol1/chapter3.htm

29. "MADD Statistics" Did You Know? Mothers Against Drunk Driving. http://www.madd-maddmetroplex.org/statistics.shtml

30. Ibid.

31. E. Eligan, Alcohol Practices, Policies and Potentials of American Colleges and Universities, Substance Abuse and Mental Health Services Administration, 2/9. http://www.ncadd.org/facts/fyibinge.html

32. B. Grant, et.al. "Prevalence of DSM-IV Alcohol Abuse and Dependence," AHRW, Vol. 18, No. 3, 1994, pp. 243, 245. http://www.ncadd.org/facts/women.html

33. Miller, TR, Levy, DT, Spicer, RS & Taylor, DM (2006) Societal costs of underage drinking *Journal of the Studies on Alcohol*, 67(4) 519–528.

34. Bishop, J.B. (2000). An environmental approach to combat binge drinking on college campuses. Journal of College Student Psychotherapy, 15, 15–30. http://www.muhlenberg.edu/mgt/presoff/alcohol/studyguide/ext_answers.html

35. Hoyert, Donna L., PhD, Heron, Melonie P., Murphy, Sherry L., BS, Kung, Hsiang-Ching, PhD; Division of Vital Statistics, "Deaths: Final Data for 2003," National Vital Statistics Reports, Vol. 54, No. 13 (Hyattsville, MD: National Center for Health Statistics, April 19, 2006), p. 5, Table C.

36. H. Wechsler et.al. "Changes in Binge Drinking and Related Problems Among American College Students Between 1993 and 1997," Journal of American College Health, Vol. 47, 9/98, p. 57. http://www.ncadd.org/facts/fyibinge.htm

37. "Substance Abuse: The Nations Number One Health Problem," Institute for Health Policy, Brandeis University, 2001. http://www.ncadd.org/facts/numberoneprob.html

38. "About Alcoholics Anonymous" The Early History of Alcoholics Anonymous. Integrity Business Systems and Solutions. http://www.about-alcoholics-anonymous.com

39. "Facts and Information" FYI Binge Drinking. The National Council on Alcoholism and Drug Dependence. http://www.ncadd.org/facts/fyibinge.htm

40. National Institute on Alcohol Abuse and Alcoholism (NIAAA), Alcohol Alert No. 29, 7/95, p. 3). http://ww.ncadd.org/facts/fyibinge.html

41. "Facts & Information" FYI Binge Drinking. The National Council on Alcoholism and Drug Dependence. http://ww.ncadd.org/facts/fyibinge.html

42. Substance Abuse and Mental Health Services Administration. Results from the 2001 National Household Survey on Drug Abuse: Volume III. Detailed Tables, last referenced 5/28/03. http://family.samhsa.gov/talk/illegaldrug.aspx

43. U.S. Department of Health & Human Services (DHHS), Office of Applied Studies, national Household Survey on Drug Abuse: Main Findings, 1997, pp. 106, 110–111. http://www.ncadd.org/facts/women.html

44. "Facts & Information" The Use of Alcohol and Other Drugs Among Women. The National Council on Alcoholism and Drug Dependence. http://www.ncadd.org/facts/women.html

45. Hingson R.W., Herren T., Zakocs R.C., Kipstein A., Wechsler H. Magnitude of Alcohol Related Mortality and Morbidity Among U.S. College Students Ages 18–24. Journal of Studies on Alcohol 63 (2): 136–144, 2002. http://www.collegedrinkingprevention.gov/statssummaries/snapshot.aspx

46. "Facts & Information" FYI Binge Drinking. The National Council on Alcoholism and Drug Dependence. http://www.ncadd.org/facts/fyibinge.html

47. "Cocaine, Statistics & Resources" Short Term Effects. Greater Dallas Council on Alcoholism and Drug Abuse. http://www.gdcada.org/statistics/cocaine/stat.htm

48. "Facts and Information" FYI Binge Drinking. The National Council on Alcoholism and Drug Dependence. http://www.ncadd.org/facts/fyibinge.html

49. Hingson R., Herren T., Zakocs R.C., Kipstein A., Wechseler H. Magnitude of Alcohol-Related Mortality and Morbidity Among U.S. College Students Ages 18–24: Changes from 1998–2001. Annual Review of Public Health, vol. 26, 259–79; 2005.

50. Hingson R., Herren T., Zakocs. R.C., Kipstein A., Wechseler H. Magnitude of Alcohol-Related Mortality and Morbidity Among U.S. College Students Ages 18–24: Journal of Studies on Alcohol 63 (2): 136–144, 2002. http://www.collegedrinkingprevention.gov/statssummaries/snapshot.aspx

51. "Facts & Information" Alcoholism and Drug Dependence are America's Number One Problem. The National Council on Alcoholism and Drug Dependence. http://www.ncadd.org/facts/numberoneprob.htm

52. "Resources" Percentage of Students Who During the Past 30 Days Rode 1 or More Times in a Vehicle Driven by Someone Who had been Drinking Alcohol. National Institute on Alcohol Abuse and Alcoholism. http://www.niaaa.nih.gov/resources/databaseresrouces/quickfacts/youth/yrbs01.htm

53. Alcohol Epidemiologic Data System. Yi, H., Chen, C.M., and Williams, G.D. Surveillance Report #76: Trends in Alcohol-Related Fatal Traffic Crashes, United States, 1982–2004. Bethesda, MD: National Institute on Alcohol Abuse and Alcoholism, Division of Epidemiology and Prevention Research (August 2006). http://www.niaaa.nih.gov/resources/databaseresourcs/quickfacts/trafficcrashes/crash13. htm

54. "Alcohol Abuse and Dependence Among U.S. College Students" John R. Knight, M.D., Henry Wechsler, Ph.D., Meichun Kuo, Sc. D., Mark Seibring B.S., Elissa R. Weitzman, Sc. D., and Marc A. Schuckit, M.D. Journal of Studies on Alcohol. 63: 3 263–270, May 2002. http://www.hsph.harvard.edu/cas/documents/dependence_0602-pressrelease

55. Substance Abuse and Mental Health Services Administration, Results from the 2006 National Survey on Drug Use and Health: National Findings, September 2007. http://www.whitehousedrugpolicy.gov/drugfact/cocaine

56. Ibid.

57. "Ecstasy Drug Use, Statistics & Effects" Drug Rehab 101. http://www.drugrehab101.com/articles101.html

58. "NIDA Info Facts: Club Drugs" National Institute on Drug Abuse (NIDA) The National Institute on Drug Abuse (NIDA) is part of the National Institutes of Health (NIH), a component of the U.S. Department of Health and Human Services. http://www.nida.nih.gov/infofacts/clubdrugs.html

59. National Institute on Drug Abuse and University of Michigan, 2006 Monitoring the Future Study Drug Data Tables, December 2006. http://www.whitehousedrugpolicy.gov/drugfact/cocaine

60. Hingson, R. et al. Magnitude of Alcohol-Related Mortality and Morbidity Among U.S. College Students Ages 18–24: Changes from 1998 to 2001. Annual Review of Public Health, vol. 26, 259–79; 2005.

61. Greenfield, Lawrence A., U.S. Department of Justice, Bureau of Justice Statistics, Alcohol and Crime: An Analysis of National Data on the Prevalence of Alcohol Involvement in Crime (Washington D.C.: U.S. Department of Justice, April 1998), p 20.

62. "NIDA Info Facts: Club Drugs" National Institute on Drug Abuse 9NIDA) The data is from NSDUH (formerly known as National Household Survey on Drug Abuse) is an annual survey of Americans age 12 and older conducted by the Substance Abuse and Mental Health Services Administration. http://www.nida.nih.gov/infofacts/clubdrugs.html

63. Drug Policy Information Clearinghouse (Office of National Drug Control Policy), Fact Sheet, November 2003.

64. Bureau of Justice Statistics, Violence in the Workplace, 1993-99, NCJ 190076, December 2001.

65. Warner, L.A., & White, H.R. (2003). Longitudinal Effects of Age at Onset and First Drinking Situations on Problem Drinking. Substance Use and Misuse, 38, 1983–2016. http://www.oas.samhsa.gov/2k4/agedependence/agedependence.htm

66. Drug Enforcement Administration (U.S. Dept. of Justice), Briefs and Background, Drugs and Drug Abuse, State Factsheet, TX, Feb. 2005.

67. "Substance Abuse: The Nations Number One Health Problem" Institute for Health Policy, Brandeis University, 1993. http://www.ncadd.org/facts/numberoneprob.htm

68. "Statistics: How Many People Have Eating Disorders?" ANRED: Anorexia Nervosa and Related Eating Disorders, Inc. http://www.anred.com/stats.html

69. Ibid.

70. Hoyert, Donna L., PhD, Heron, Melonie P., PhD, Murphy, Sherry L., BS, Kung, Hsiang-Ching, PhD; Division of Vital Statistics, "Deaths: Final Data for 2003," National Vital Statistics Reports, Vol. 54, No. 13 (Hyattsville, MD: National Center for Health Statistics, April 19, 2006), p. 10.

71. "Membership" Welcome to Alcoholics Anonymous. Alcoholics Anonymous World Services, Inc. www.aa.org

72. "Membership Demographics" Information about NA 2007. Narcotics Anonymous World Services, Inc. http://www.na.org/basic.htm

73. Hill, S.Y. Biological Consequences of Alcoholism and Alcohol-Related Problems Among Women. In: Special Populations Issues. National Institute on Alcohol Abuse and Alcoholism. Alcohol and Health Monograph No. 4 DHHS Pub. No. 9ADM) 82–1193. Washington, D.C.: Supt. of Docs., U.S. Govt. Print. Off., 1982. Pp 43–73. http://www.marininstitute.org/alcohol_policy/women_alcohol.htm

74. National Institute of Mental Health (NIMH). "The Numbers Count: Mental Illness in America," Science on Our Minds Fact Sheet Series. http://www.upliftprogram.com/depression_facts.html

75. NIMH. "The Numbers Count: Mental Illness in America," Science on Our Minds Fact Sheet Series. http://www.upliftprogram.com/depression)facts.html

76. Agency for Healthcare Research and Quality, 2003. "National Healthcare Quality Report." This is a widely quoted statistic, though some experts such as Dr. Christopher L. Summerville, Executive Director of the Manitoba Schizophrenia Society, member of the Board of Directors of Mood Disorders of Canada, have cited higher figures. http://www.upliftprogram.com/depression_facts.html

77. "National Healthcare Quality Report," 2003. http://www.upliftprogram.com/depression_facts.html

78. "The Societal Promise of Improving Care for Depression" Research Highlights. Objective Analysis and Effective Solutions. RAND Corporation. http://www.rand.org/pubs/research_briefs/rb9055/index1.html

79. Deborah Lott, "Childhood Trauma, CRF Hypersecretion and Depression," Psychiatric Times, October 1999, 16 (10); Danya Glaser, "Child Abuse and Neglect and the Brain," J Child Psychol. & Psychiatry. 2000, 41: 1:91–116.

80. Patricia L. Owens, Valerie Slaymaker, J. Scott Tonigan, Barbara S. McCrady, Elizabeth E. Epstein, Lee Ann Kaskutas, Keith Humphreys, William R. Miller., "Participation in Alcoholics Anonymous: Intended and Unintended Change Mechanisms," Alcoholism: Clinical and Experimental Research. Vol. 27, Issue 3, Page 524, March 2003. http://www.blackwell-synergy.com/toc/acer/27/3

81. Anne Katherine. Boundaries: Where You End and I Begin. Hazelden, MJF Books, Fine Communications. 1991. Pg 35.

82. American Association of Suicidology, "Some Facts About Suicide in the U.S.A." 2001. http://www.211bigbend.org/hotlines/suicide/statistics.htm

83. "Teen Drug Use" Statistics on Teenage Drug Use. Teen Help LLC. http://www.teendrugabuse.us/teen_drug_use.html

84. American Association of Suicidology, "Some Facts About Suicide in the U.S.A." 2001. http://www.211bigbend.org/hotlines/suicide/statistics.htm

85. Ronald C. Kessler. Alcohol Fuels Suicidal Tendencies. WOR Health Center. October 2002.

86. Drinking in the United States: Main Findings from the 1992 National Longitudinal Alcohol Epidemiologic Survey, National Institute on Alcohol Abuse and Alcoholism, 11/98. http://www.ncadd.org/facts/fyidina.html

87. Substance Abuse and Mental Health Services Administration, Treatment Episode Data Set (TEDS) Highlights—2005, February 2007. http://www.whitehousedrugpolicy.gov/drugfact/women/index.html#go10

88. Substance Abuse: The Nation's Number One Health Problem, Overview: The Context of Substance Abuse. Schneider Institute for Health Policy. Brandeis University for the Robert Wood Johnson Foundation, February 2007.

89. Position Paper on Drug Policy, Physician Leadership on National Drug Policy (PLNDP), Brown University Center for Alcohol and Addiction Studies, 2000. http://www.ncadd.og/facts/numberoneprob.html#6

90. "Substance Abuse: The Nation's Number One Health Problem," Institute for Health Policy, Brandeis University, 2001. http://www.ncadd.org/facts/numberoneprob.html

91. "Full Report: Worker Substance Use and Workplace Policies and Programs" SAMHSA, Office of Applied Science. July 2007. http://oas.samhsa.gov/work2k7/toc.cfm

92. Ibid.

93. Ibid.

94. "About.com: Alcoholism," Denial-A Symptom of Alcoholism? August 2007. http://alcoholism.about.com/cs/info2/a/aa050797.htm

95. WHO Report on Mental Illness Released October 4, 2001. Health News Stories: Depression Link to heart Disease, Hostility, Depression May Boost Heart Disease. http://www.upliftprogram.com/depression_facts.html

96. "Addiction Overview and Strategy" The Problem. Robert Wood Johnson Foundation, 2007. http://www.rwjf.org/pr/os.jsp?topicid=1006

97. Greenfield, Lawrence A., U.S. Department of Justice Bureau of Statistics, Alcohol and Crime: An Analysis of National Data on Prevalence of Alcohol Involvement in Crime (Washington, D.C.: U.S. Department of Justice, April 1998), p. 20.

98. The National Survey on Drug Use and Health (NSDUH) 2002, 2003, 2004. Department of Health and Human Services, Substance Abuse and Mental Health Services Association.

99. "Mental Illness Research Association" Statistics on Suicide. MIRA. National Institute of Mental Health. 2002. http://www.miraresearch.org/understanding/statistics.htm

100. S. Wilsnack, et.al., "How Women Drink: Epidemiology of Women's Drinking and Problem Drinking,"National Institute on Alcohol Abuse and Alcoholism (NIAA), Alcohol Health and Research World (AHRW), Vol. 18 No. 3, 1994, p. 176.

101. U.S. Department of Health and Human Services. SAMHSA's Center for Substance Abuse Prevention. Prevention Alert: The Binge Drinking Epidemic (Volume 5, Number 6 ed.) Washington D.C.: U.S. Government Printing Office. http://ncadi.samhsa.gov/govpubs/prevalert/v5/2.aspx

Sources

The statistics and information found in this book were gathered from a wide range of sources including the following…

Greater Council on Alcoholism & Drug Addiction
www.gdcada.org

Mothers Against Drunk Driving
www.madd.org

National Council on Alcoholism & Drug Dependence
www.ncadd.org

National Institute on Alcohol Abuse & Alcoholism
www.niaaa.nih.gov

National Institute on Drug Abuse
www.nida.nih.gov

National Institute on Mental Health
www.nimh.nih.gov

About the Author

Miss Amy "AJ" Crowell holds a Bachelor in Business Administration, a Masters in Business Administration, and a secondary teaching certification in Career & Technology. She is a recovered alcoholic and drug addict and has been alcohol and drug free since April 19, 1988.

Amy is an expert on alcoholism and drug addiction because of her personal experience and in-depth knowledge of the disease. She is a phenomenal motivational speaker and often addresses a variety of audiences including high schools, colleges, corporations, conventions, seminars and private meetings. Amy is a natural at public speaking and when she enters a room her vivacious personality and energy immediately draws attention. Her smile is infectious and her positive attitude radiates and touches everyone around her.

For the last several years, she has been a high school teacher in Dallas and taught economically disadvantaged and at-risk students. Amy is zealous about working with young people and educating them on addictions. She strives to help young adults avoid her addiction experiences. The unconditional love that she genuinely has for other people is heartwarming.

Goals are mandatory for Amy so she can direct her energy fulfilling her dreams. Her life-time goal is to educate millions of people about alcoholism and drug addiction. She is currently working on several other books for publication and will be releasing her newest creation called *Calm, Cool & Connected to Positive Thinking!*

AJC Media Services
3333 W. Campbell Road #361
Richardson, TX 75090
www.amycrowell.net
information@amycrowell.net

www.ingramcontent.com/pod-product-compliance
Lightning Source LLC
Chambersburg PA
CBHW060504290526
45791CB00001B/255
9781419656040